CW00411280

Contents

What you need to know before you buy this book

This book is like me. Imperfect and average. It doesn't show great literary skill. You will not be blown away by my writing style. But hopefully you will be blown away by the messages inside.

I have written this book to convey all the lessons, messages, knowledge and understanding that I wish I had had as I faced my life's ups and downs.

I am sharing it in the hope it will help YOU as you face YOUR life's ups and downs.

This book is the exact length it needs to be. That means it is shorter than a 'standard' book (whatever that is), but it isn't padded out with unnecessary fluff to make it a certain length. I value my time and yours more than that.

Should you buy this book?

DON'T buy this book if you expect it to be perfectly written. You will be disappointed.

DON'T buy this book if you are not prepared to read it with an open mind, and are convinced that nothing anyone says or does will change things for you.
DO buy this book if you're willing to take a risk and learn from someone else's failures and falls, and what they learnt along the way.

DO buy this book if you want to be entertained and inspired. If you want to be happier in your life, to see change in the way you live, parent, work and in the way you experience relationships.

DO buy this book if you like audiobooks as there is an option to download the audio version for free inside.

Praise & reviews for *How to be happy…*

"It's taken me just an hour and 10 minutes to read your book, Sophie. You've taken me from tears to laughter and through all of your highs and lows. I loved every page and am sure it will inspire many more ladies to believe in themselves and follow their dreams. You are amazing and thank you for everything you do."
Jennifer Chamberlin - founder of My Bilingual VA and mum of 2 almost teenagers

"I just finished your book...I LOVED reading it. I LOVED that you shared so much with us so freely and willingly. It's an amazing and inspirational read. Women all over the world will enjoy sharing your journey and learning through your life experiences. You are truly amazing."
Denise Pitot - founder of Mauritius Business Network and mum of 3

"I started reading it this morning and can't put it down. It's brill!...I have just landed and spent the whole flight reading your book! I've finished it! It is absolutely fan-bloody-tastic! It was funny, sad and inspirational all at the same time, which I LOVE in a book!"
Tracey Maurin - English teacher and mum of 2

"One of the things I loved about your book was the chapter titles: 'The one where..., the one when...' It was such an easy book to read and I could relate to so many parts of it. The ones where I couldn't relate, like your miscarriage and the violent boyfriend, I thought of those women out there who will benefit so much from these testimonials and how you dealt with them. It was really nice to read that even you, Sophie Le Brozec, wanted to eBay Léna. I wanna eBay my kids most days of the week ☺"
Olivia D.B. - mum of 2

"I love hearing people's back stories and exactly what made them who they are and brought them to where they are today, and yours is no exception! Love your honesty and the fact that you didn't shy away from some intensely personal experiences and your feelings about them, then and now. There's plenty for ANY woman to identify with, whether it's about your love life, family life, work life or good old cultural differences. It's a roller coaster of a read!"
Jac R-F - mum of one

Tracey Maurin went into more detail about her thoughts on *How to be Happy:*

I like the way you've used the "Friends" titles for each chapter, it comes across as original and not boring ("The one with / where….").

Some of the things that made me laugh out loud:

- Jane the sex beast!
- Russian ballet dancer handshake!
- The fact that French TV is indeed so shit!
- Wanting to eBay Léna (I also think your honesty here was brilliant as SO many of us have been / go through this and think we're bad parents for having these thoughts)
- Mooing in labour with your lardy arse and cellulite thighs! (Again, brutal honesty to make you relatable and reassuring to real women)
- The pelvic floor description in France whilst discussing Christmas plans!

I love the way that you are so honest in the book which so many people will appreciate and relate to and find comfort in, especially:

- The shouty mummy
- Your honesty in the very troubled period in your marriage and losing yourself
- It was heart-breaking reading about your miscarriage and it gave me a clearer understanding as to how women are massively affected by this.
- It made me well up reading the Life Reboot Camp feedback about saving marriages – what you do is amazing.
- I loved the advice about watching kids while they sleep when they are going through very challenging phases.
- I loved the bit about when you got to Mauritius and Priscille turned up with a welcome basket – it made me feel all warm inside and I fell in love with Priscille who I don't even know!
- Even though I have read about your journey through your blog, it was lovely reading it all in detail.

Dedication

**This book is dedicated to
all the incredible women
in the online courses I run, especially
Life Reboot Camp**.
You amazing, wonderful, beautiful, loving ladies
are my sisters, my family,
my community, my world.
Thank you for saying yes to me,
and all my crazy, swearing, imperfect ways.
I might have changed your lives,
but you change mine too.
For the better. Every day.

Introduction

I want you to get the most out of this book as possible. I want you to take away tools that help you to be happy, no matter what shit life throws at you. So there are task chapters with clear action steps that you can take. But to make it even easier I have created a set of free bonuses to accompany this book:

1. A PDF of all the task chapters in one easy-to-access document.
2. A simple checklist of how to be happy for you to print out and refer back to on tough days.
3. An audio version of the book (in case you prefer listening to reading).
4. A motivational "kick up the rear" audio from me, to listen to when you need a pick-me-up.

To access all these free book bonuses just head to www.SophieLeBrozec.com/happy-bonus

Just in case that isn't enough, all readers of *How to be happy…* can also sign up to my signature online programme and community, **Life Reboot Camp**, and get lifetime access at a reduced rate. I talk about Life Reboot Camp in the book, but please, if this appeals to you, don't sign up via the usual link on my website or you'll pay full price. For all the information about LRC and to sign up at a lower rate, head to www.SophieLeBrozec.com/camp-book

How to read this book

How to be happy… is part memoir and part personal development and is written in chronological order. The memoir chapters all start "The one…" (you might recognise this from the TV series 'Friends') and the personal development chapters all start "Task". You can either read from start to finish or you can dip in and out based on what interests you / what you need help with at any given moment.

All the early readers have told me it's a quick and easy book to read which was my goal, I hope you find this to be the case too.

Prologue

As I floated in the warm turquoise waters, looking at the clear blue sky above me, the beautiful island in front of me with its picture postcard beach and at the wonderful friends surrounding me I mentally pinched myself.

"This is my life. This is my actual fucking life!" I repeated in my head, as I couldn't quite believe it.

What had been the world's biggest pipe dream when I was 17, and had evolved into a daydream in my late 30s was now my reality. I was literally living my dream.

Here I was, with the love of my life and 20 great friends on a boat trip, drinking rum punch, jumping into the clearest and warmest water, swimming in what felt like an aquarium, and feeling such joy I could burst.

It had been a long journey to get here. I had had to hit rock bottom. Several times. Suffer some real valleys to be able to enjoy the peaks, but I had finally arrived at the place I was always meant to be.

In a body I loved. In a life I loved. Surrounded by people I loved. In a place I loved. Doing work I loved. For the first time in my life I felt like I had really made it.

All the pain, tears, anger, frustration and depression that had come before were all worth it. I now appreciate every day, with its inevitable highs and lows. I appreciate every single wonderful thing that I have and that I have achieved in this one beautiful, brutal life. Or as Glennon Doyle so succinctly puts it, in this one "brutiful life".

The one with the abusive relationship

As he viciously kicked the magazine rack into the wall, creating a hole, I floated up above my body and wondered who I was and how the hell I'd got here. I tried to console him but he turned to me in a rage.

"What do you fucking know?!"

Experience had told me the best thing was to get his drunken 6 foot something body to bed and let him sleep it off, but I wasn't sure I could. I was tired. Tired of permanently being on edge, waiting for the next eruption. Wondering if the physical violence might overflow to me one of these days.

I gently suggested he go upstairs while I made him some food to bring up. He'd not eaten all day and I was hoping that the prospect of waitress service might coax him to his room, where hopefully he would pass out almost immediately.

He reluctantly agreed and I guided him upstairs as his footing was unstable after a day of drinking. I helped lie him down on the bed promising to be back very soon with a plate full of food.

As I entered the kitchen I asked myself again how I had got here. Less than a year previously I had been in a loving relationship with one of the nicest guys I know, but some kind of crazy teen / young adult hormones had kicked in and pushed me to rebel, ending that relationship in favour of one with an abusive loser.

I disgusted myself. I was the exact kind of woman I'd always looked down on. I mean how stupid do you have to be to stay in a relationship with a man who's abusing you? Whether it's physical or emotional. But now I knew. Now I understood.

You see they are very clever. When you first meet them they are charming and they work like a drug - you get sucked in quickly and even though the comedown of being with them hurts, you keep going back for the next hit, you want to recapture that charm and excitement of the early days.

And once you're in their trap you get entangled further and further every day. Your outfits get chosen for you. Not literally but it becomes too hard to argue with "don't wear that - it makes you look fat / ugly / like a slut", so you wear what he wants you to in order to keep the peace.

You argue when it's time for you to meet up with friends outside of his circle. Because he can't control that. So the first time - when you're still feeling strong and self-confident from the old you - you say "screw you!" and you go to see your friend, but when you get back he is upset, in tears, and makes you feel bad about going. You say you won't go next time, and you apologise.

He repeats this with every friend and family member that he doesn't know or who he has no control over, either threatening to leave you, forbidding you to go or crying when you do go. Until it becomes easier to just cut ties with everyone or reduce them to the absolute minimum.

Next up he works on what he says to make sure it hits you the hardest.

"You're so ugly, it's just as well I'm with you as no other fucker would want you!"

The first time you yell back "fuck you!" as you know it's not true. How dare he?! The next time you tell him to shut up, and you look at yourself in the mirror, zooming in on all the bits you hate about your face and body. By the third time you are so tightly caught up in his web that all you can think is "I know I'm ugly, please don't leave me!".

So when he goes crazy, kicking furniture and denting walls because Liverpool lost the FA Cup football match, and you wonder if you're going to be the next one to be hit, you just try and calm things down, you don't ever think of leaving him.

When he spends all evening in the pub chatting to and flirting with his ex-girlfriend, then disappears from the house you've gone home to together, to go to her, spending all night there, you don't dare say much. First there is the fear of his temper, then there is the far bigger fear that he might leave you, because you've already established that you are worth less than nothing.

Your friends have faded away, you've cancelled on them too many times and they've moved on as they can't stand him, and don't like or recognise the person you have become with him. This shell of your former self. Even if you wanted to get out there is no one left, you are no one and have no one without him.

For me this went on for a bit more than a year, although it felt far longer at the time. He knew how strong I'd been originally, and knew how hard it would be to hang on to me so, as I was getting ready to move to France for the third year of my university degree, he stepped up the pressure. He wanted us to get married, for me to get pregnant, as then he could fully control me. Luckily for me there was still a nucleus of Sophie left inside of me somewhere that refused to give up my university dream. That knew that marriage and babies with him was a really bad idea.

I didn't know, as I stood at Heathrow airport with two of my university friends saying goodbye to our parents, that this was my way out. I didn't realise as I got on that Air France flight that this was the passageway to my freedom. It scares the crap out of me now to think what might have happened if I hadn't had that escape route. Because university over 200 miles away in the UK hadn't been enough to break us up. Thankfully nearly 3 months in France with very limited communication did the trick.

As a mum of two daughters I am so fearful of them falling into the same trap. I was so strong, sure of myself, self-confident, happy in my own skin, that I never should have fallen prey to someone like him. But I did, so I aim to be hyper vigilant with my girls as they get older.

Task - how to deal with toxic relationships and friendships

You don't have to be in an abusive relationship to have people saying things about you that aren't true. The problem is, as Julia Roberts says in Pretty Woman,

Vivian:
People put you down enough, you start to believe it.

Edward Lewis:
I think you are a very bright, very special woman.

Vivian:
The bad stuff is easier to believe.

Here are two facts for you:

1. There will always be people who want to put you down and say negative things about you, whether it is out there or a veiled insult. This is a fact of life.
2. The bad stuff will always be easier to believe.

So what can you do about it?

First of all, do your absolute best to only surround yourself with people who light you up, who lift you up, who want the best for you, who cheer you when you win and commiserate when you fail. Anyone else does not deserve a seat at your table. If you have people in your life who do not fall into this category of lifting and lighting you up then you need to think carefully about putting some distance between you.

Next, remember that anyone saying something negative is probably a person who is not in a great place. That insult likely comes from a place of jealousy, fear, lack of self-confidence or something similar. It is unlikely it has much to do with you. My abusive ex insulted me out of fear that I would leave him, and because he wanted to control me. It was never about me.

If you recognise that you are in a toxic relationship or friendship, please do whatever you can to leave it. Ask for help from friends or loved ones, look online for organisations, and if you're really stuck message me on social media (just look for Sophie Le Brozec), I'll see if I can point you in the right direction.

When there are people you can't separate yourself from (neighbours, colleagues, in-laws etc) there are some things you can put into practice to protect yourself:

- Avoid them as much as possible. Problems with your mother-in-law? Let your husband see his mum without you. Issues with your best friend's boyfriend? Arrange to have girls only nights out.
- When you do see them brace yourself in advance. Remind yourself that these nasty comments are about the other person,

not you. Prep yourself for typical comments you are likely to receive, and maybe prepare a calm response, or decide where you can escape to (the toilet / check on the children / a breath of fresh air etc).

- Afterwards plan something nice to look forward to - a long soak in the bath, a catch-up with a good friend, trashy TV, your favourite chocolate bar etc.

There are toxic people out there but you don't need to have them all in your life, and there are ways to deal with them. You can do this lovely. (This is something I cover in Life Reboot Camp too.)

Don't forget if you would like easy access to all the tasks in this book, along with a checklist and an audio to keep your spirits high, just head to www.SophieLeBrozec.com/happy-bonus and grab all your free bonuses.

The one where I moved to France for 3 months & stayed for 12 years

I'd barely finished university and suddenly everyone wanted to know what I was going to do with my life. The thing was I honestly didn't have a clue. From the age of 8 I'd known that I was going to go to university to study French; we had gone to France on a family holiday and I had fallen in love with the country and the language, also I turned out to be a bit of a linguist.

When I was 17 I applied to various universities to study French and Spanish. When people asked me what I was going to do afterwards I would jokingly say "move to a French-speaking tropical island". It was only ever a joke as in 1993 that was pretty much an impossibility, which just goes to show that even impossible dreams can come true...

I assumed that by the time I graduated I would know EXACTLY what I wanted to do with my life. But I was wrong, and I was lost.

I knew what I DIDN'T want to do. I didn't want to be a teacher. I hate rules and I knew I would never be able to enforce stupid school rules if I became a French teacher. I also didn't want to be a translator (the other classic career path after a language degree). Studying the critique of translation at university had completely knocked any translation dreams out of my head. Also I was very average and I was afraid I wasn't good enough.

I had a 2:2 degree in French and Spanish from university, and if you're not aware of the grading system of UK universities there are 4 possible grades you can pass with - this is the 3rd out of 4. Definitely no genius. So WHAT was I going to do?

No one seemed to know or be able to help. Careers advisors at university told me that half of language students work in jobs that have nothing to do with languages. That was a big, fat NO for me. I studied languages because I loved them and wanted to use them in my everyday life.

I went to a Careers Fair, excited at the prospects available to me. There were two potential employers who wanted my languages - Decathlon sports shop and GCHQ. After being a Saturday girl in shops from the age of 14 I knew that Decathlon was a no, as was GCHQ as I knew I wanted to be ordinary, settle down, get married and have kids, and that being a spy probably wouldn't fit in well with that.

So I left university and moved back in with my parents, still lost. I had a 3 month trip to Nice booked with two of my friends. We had met the summer before when I was living there as a student and had decided to head back for a summer of fun. Whenever anyone asked what I was going to do after my summer blow-out I would tell them "oh you know, the usual, marriage, mortgage, kids", as it really felt like my life as I knew it was over. My fun years were behind me I believed, now it was time to adult until I died. It wasn't a great prospect but I just thought that was life.

Then I got to Nice and it was a breath of fresh air. Nobody cared what plans I had for the future. I spent my days, well it was my nights actually as I was working in a bar until 3am 6 days a week, with expats from all over the world who weren't too worried about futures or careers.

Life was all about living. It was slave labour but I was having a ball. I lived in a one bedroom apartment with my 2 friends - two of us shared the bedroom and the third slept on a sofa bed in the lounge.

We all worked nights in bars, went out and partied after, then collapsed into bed sometime around dawn, falling into a drunken slumber, getting up in the afternoon for a few hours on the beach before doing it all over again. I worked 6 days a week, 9 hours a night for an absolute pittance, way below minimum wage, all paid in cash, hush hush, as it was completely illegal.

But for the most part we didn't care. We were young, we were (mostly) having fun - except for being groped by drunk customers and having to clean vomit out of toilets at 2am. The "what are you going to do with your life now?" questions were nowhere to be heard, and that suited me perfectly.

Within about a week of this lifestyle my friends and I came to the realisation we had no reason or need to leave Nice after 3 months. We had return tickets but we had just graduated, and had no jobs, homes or boyfriends to go back for. So we decided to stay on in Nice. Indefinitely.

I finally left Nice and moved back to the UK 12 years and 18 days after I arrived there. This time I had a husband, a 3 year old daughter, a dog and a cat in tow.

Task - how to figure out what to do with your life

I seriously wish I'd known at 22 what I know now about figuring out what to do with your life. No one was capable of or interested in giving me any actual advice about what options were open to me. I have finally arrived at my dream life and dream career after 20 years of trial and error. Hopefully this task will help you avoid that.

It's quite simple to figure out what to do with your life if you want to be happy. (If you just want to make money and you don't care about being happy when you work feel free to skip this section.)

1. Grab a decent-sized piece of paper and a pen
2. Write down a list of all the things you LIKE doing
3. Write down a list of all the things you are GOOD at
4. Write down your FINANCIAL obligations / how much money you need or want to earn every month or year

Now have a look at where you have overlaps. If you like writing and are good at writing, start Googling things like "what job can you do that involves writing?" and have a look at the different salary options to check it fits your 'financial' list. (We go into this exercise in more detail in Life Reboot Camp.)

If you'd like an easy-to-access PDF of all the tasks in this book head to www.SophieLeBrozec.com/happy-bonus to download it and all the other free book bonuses.

The one with the reality of working in France

Do you know how difficult it is to get a decent job in France? Ridiculously hard. Actually it's probably just as well I didn't know or I probably would have gone back to the UK, tail between my legs before even trying.

I decided that if I was going to stay in France then I wanted to get a 'proper' job and not stay working as a barmaid forever. Everyone thought I was crazy, but I'd lived in Nice during the winter as a student, and I knew that my summertime lifestyle wouldn't be quite as fun once the tourists went home. So I went about looking for work. Back in 1998 it was a full-time job.

I don't know what it's like now but back then you had to handwrite your application letter, and there were a zillion rules about the words and phrases you had to use. Choose the wrong expression or use it incorrectly and your application went straight in the bin. Apparently the handwritten letter was so that they could analyse your handwriting and see if you were the right kind of person for the job.

On top of that your CV was the equivalent of sticking a middle finger up at feminists. You HAD to add a photo of yourself to your CV, give your date of birth and state your marital status. I mean, what the actual fuck?!?

And you know what? Once I was on the other side of the recruitment desk I saw how many women got jobs based on marital status and looks. Scary! In a later job I took over from a woman who'd been employed on looks alone and was incapable of doing the job. They ended up terminating her contract at great expense, wasting so much company time and money, just because the boss fancied her and offered her the job for that one reason.

Luckily for me I quickly found out that he wasn't interested in me in the same way; one day a friend of his came for lunch and, on seeing me at my desk, asked my boss "have you changed your PA?" to which my boss replied "yeah, I already made the mistake of employing based on beauty, this time I've gone for brains". I cannot tell you how delighted I was to hear that!

Anyway I digress. So there I was, in 1998, looking for a job, handwriting my application letters, getting passport photos done again and again, searching in the *Nice Matin* local newspaper. And hearing crickets.

It turns out that in France everyone has a degree. It doesn't make you anything special. And to add insult to injury a language degree is pretty much bottom of the pile. So I had very little going for me. I applied for anything and everything that I thought I might stand a chance of getting. But heard nothing back. Not even rejection letters.

I could have gone back to the UK. Time was ticking by. I had very little money and I knew I would get a job back home overnight, but I really wasn't ready to leave France yet.

After weeks spent job-hunting I finally scored myself an interview. I was ridiculously excited. I wasn't really sure what the job itself was, but it didn't matter, I would have taken anything at that stage.

The interview was in a rented office space and I was ushered into an office where I met my future boss.

He was small (I'm barely 5 foot 4 inches so that's saying something) and round, bald with small, gappy, brown teeth which he was beaming at me with. I could see and feel him looking me up and down, like I was some kind of racehorse he was going to purchase. But I didn't care. I needed that job. That job would keep me in France.

He asked next to no questions about my typing speed, if I was any good at taking minutes at meetings, or anything else you might ask a potential secretary, which is what the role seemed to be. Instead he asked me how long I'd been in Nice, and - most importantly - if I was really "*célibataire*" (single) as my CV stated.

With my confirmation that I was indeed not in a relationship he offered me the job there and then, even taking me out to lunch after the interview. The contract was a good one too - a 'CDI' (*Contrat à durée indéterminée*) which are like gold dust, as basically you've got the job for life, or they have to pay you a hefty sum of money if they want to get rid of you. It was also a good monthly salary for France at the time - 7,500 francs (approximately $1,250). It was a pittance for me after my student temping jobs just outside of London but, as I was told by many French friends, a great salary for me and my crappy CV.

And that was that. I finally had my job. I discovered over the next few weeks and months that French employers are not the fastest at replying to job applications. Little by little rejection letters and offers of interviews trickled in. For jobs that I had applied for 3-4 months previously sometimes!

But it didn't matter, I had signed my CDI and I was safe. I had my job for life, I could relax and enjoy myself again. Or so I thought….

The one where my boss was arrested

Life is never as smooth as it seems or as we might hope. The job started off terribly but quickly got better. The first few days I had to go and work at my boss's house. It was me, him and his housekeeper, and I had to get the bus there. Which is fine. Except the bus stop was in *L'Ariane*, at the time the most notoriously dangerous area of Nice. Where the police and fire brigade rarely even ventured.

That didn't bode well but fortunately he told me it was temporary and soon we were moving to offices near the airport (safer and easier) with other employees (huzzah, colleagues to hang out with!).

Before all that there was going to be a big seminar near Lyon. I didn't really understand what it was all about at the time. I was 22 and didn't have a clue about the world of business. Later on I realised that he was sweet-talking potential investors. BIG investors. So no expense was spared.

We were in the same hotel where the recent world cup-winning French football team had stayed in the lead-up to that summer's championship. My hotel "room" was bigger than the apartment I had been sharing with my two friends when we first arrived in Nice. Every meal was 4-5 courses with red wine and champagne flowing constantly. I hated red wine before that job but I quickly grew to like it as I was given so much of it. Also, drinking really really decent red wine probably helps too!

I was completely lost during the whole 48 hours we were there. I didn't know what the business was about - partly because it was very vague and partly because I was quickly realising that a degree in

French does not make you fluent. Also I was surrounded by *grown-ups*. I was 22, and had only just stopped my hedonistic lifestyle of bar work, party hard, beach bum.

Luckily my boss had also hired a PA who saved my life while I worked for him. Caroline was half-English and half-French and, at 11 years my senior, was like a protective aunt for me. She spoke to me in English (the relief after hours of trying to follow fast-flowing French conversations) and explained what she knew about the business and what to expect. We quickly became sisters in arms and had fun together, laughing and chatting at work, and looking out for each other.

I will always remember three things that stood out for me about office work in France, coming from the UK. I might have only been 22 but every university holiday I had temped in offices, from those with single figure staff to the UK head office of Panasonic, so I did know a thing or two about office work.

What shocked me about office work in France was this - everyone smoked IN their office. It was 1998 and this was completely normal; all my colleagues had ashtrays on their desks, alongside their computer keyboard.

Next up was the office culture. You know the way in the UK it is not shocking at all - actually it's pretty normal - to go out for after-work drinks on a Friday with colleagues? When I suggested this to my colleagues they all looked at me like I was a raging alcoholic. I didn't ask twice.

The last thing was French office vocabulary, in my defence this came up just after my going out for drinks suggestion. A colleague came into my office one day and asked me if I had any scotch…. I didn't know how to reply. Did he think I had a bottle of whisky hidden in my desk drawer because of my Friday drinks suggestion? But it was 11am. I decided to try and find out more.

"What do you mean do I have any scotch? What scotch?!" I asked.

After a bit of miming from him I quickly realised that scotch in France was NOTHING to do with alcohol, but was in fact sellotape, as in scotch tape! Just as well I didn't get all defensive about not being a raging alcoholic, despite what they might think.

Whilst all of this was a bit of a shock, and a difference from office work in the UK it was nothing in comparison to what was to come next…

It was a Friday evening and I was sitting down to watch TV at home. I had the local news on to try and improve my French and suddenly I saw my boss, in handcuffs, being dragged into the courthouse in Nice.

I was all "what the FUCK?!?" but there was no one for me to talk this over with and it was several years before the joys of being able to Google this kind of stuff. My flatmates / friends were both out working (they had also decided to stay in Nice, and were still doing bar work) and my friendship with Caroline hadn't yet progressed to exchanging phone numbers. There was nothing for it, I was going to have to sit in my apartment, drinking cheap French wine, and repeating to myself over and over "what the fuck?! What the fuck?!" until Monday morning.

"I saw our boss in handcuffs on the local news on Friday night!" I burst out to Caroline as soon as she walked into the office.

"What does it mean?" I whined. Not my best moment but I'd been stewing over this all weekend.

She did her best to reassure me as we went to see another colleague, Fabrice, who knew our boss better, having worked with him a fair few times in the past.

It turned out that this was archived footage and nothing new, so he hadn't suddenly been arrested since leaving the office on Friday. Fabrice tried to calm us both by explaining that some journalists on the local news had it in for our boss, and dragged this footage out from time to time to get at him.

Hmmmm, ok, but that didn't change the fact that I'd seen him in handcuffs, being dragged into the courthouse. It wasn't made up. It had actually happened. Just not this weekend.

Fabrice brushed this all off as being nothing major, but in my gut I knew there was something very off with my boss and this company.

It turned out that our boss had been involved in some rather dodgy business activity a few years previously, had been arrested for fraud and was no longer allowed to practise business in France. This explained why our work contracts were signed with a company in Luxembourg, not France, and with a female CEO, who it turned out was our boss's mistress. All very French I thought.

I would love to share more about exactly what happened but my former boss is an incredibly rich and powerful man, with links to the Russian Mafia, and is still just as dodgy business-wise as he was back in 1998-1999. So I daren't say anymore.

This information from Fabrice sowed a seed of doubt in mine and Caroline's minds. This all sounded a bit suspicious and wrong. So moving forwards we kept our eyes open.

Shortly after, a sales and marketing manager was employed for the company in Paris; he started to find out things about our boss and then received death threats before finally handing in his notice. Caroline started to ask questions and was promptly fired - meaning our boss would have to pay her a large sum as you can't fire people easily in France.

As for me, I was 23 and way too young to be caught up in Russian Mafia, death threats, fraudulent bosses and other crazy shit. Not to mention my sleazeball boss would constantly say how much he wanted to get together with me, and shout at me that I'd lied about being single on my CV. Untrue. I was single when I applied for the job but then met my first French boyfriend around the time I started working for the company. This did not go down well.

But I felt stuck. I didn't have a job to go to. I knew how hard it was to find work in France. I wouldn't be entitled to unemployment benefit if I resigned, but I knew I couldn't carry on working for that downright frightening and odious man. So I handed in my notice. I didn't expect the reaction I got. My boss roared at me. Actually roared, told me I was ungrateful, after everything he had done for me (I'm still not sure what that was, other than offer me a job and pay me an ok salary….). It was scary as fuck, because at this stage I knew what he was capable of. But I held firm. I had a month's notice to work and then I was leaving.

Interestingly a few years later I did some simultaneous translation work for the BBC in Nice. They were filming a programme with Jeremy Clarkson and I had to translate his interview with an investigative journalist, who was talking to Clarkson about the Russian Mafia in Nice. When I told the journalist off camera who my ex-boss was he was desperate to find out what I knew, but I was still too scared to share much.

This first grown-up job had also made me realise that I was bored out of my brains. Every morning when my alarm went off I would snooze it as long as I possibly could, whilst counting down the days until the weekend and the years until I could retire. Honestly. So I decided to apply for a different kind of job this time. Languages had always been my passion, but I couldn't do anything with French in France. Instead I switched my attention to my own language, and started looking at language schools where I could teach English as a foreign language.

I had no qualifications to teach, no TEFL (Teaching English as a Foreign Language) certificate but I knew languages, had done some basic French teaching at university and knew I was good at it. With that knowledge I put myself out into the world. I didn't wait to answer job ads this time, I got out the yellow pages and applied to every language school in Nice. Then within a few days of sending out my CV and application letter I rang the schools.

One day I hit jackpot. I rang the day one of their teachers resigned. Long story short I got the job and in a few weeks I hung up my secretary hat and donned my teacher hat.

Task - how to get the job you want

I was in my early twenties, in a job I absolutely hated, that held no interest for me except it paid my rent and bills. Every morning I was snoozing my alarm clock and counting down the years until I could retire.

If you are living anything vaguely resembling this then please take this as a wake-up call. It doesn't have to be this way and you are wasting a damn good life putting up with this crap.

Because I didn't want to work for my scary Russian-mafia-related boss anymore I was desperate, which also made me think about things differently.

First of all I knew I wanted a job that interested me, not one where I hated my alarm clock. So I got really clear on what that might be (go back to the chapter "Task - how to figure out what to do with your life" if you're not sure on this one). Next I knew I didn't have time to wait for jobs to become available and advertised, I needed to be PROactive not REactive.

To get the job you want here's what to do:

1. Figure out what that is (go back to the last task if need be) and be REALISTIC. Your dream job might be a professional ballet

dancer, but if you are 38 years old and have never danced in your life you might need to think again.

2. Having said that, don't be afraid to change industries, to take a pay cut (if you can make it work for you financially), to start from the bottom again, to retrain, to go back to studying. Later on in the book I'll explain about retraining when I was 37 years old, and it was the best thing ever for me, so don't discard the idea.

3. Make sure your CV, LinkedIn profile etc are up to date with this new job you want to go for.

4. Go out and look for jobs in that industry / that role. Approach companies where you'd like to work. Get on people's radar. Ask friends / family if they have any connections that could help you. Talk about your wish to change roles / industries on LinkedIn, explain why, what you bring to the table and ask people to share. It's a great network for this kind of thing. Go to networking events in your area and see who you meet that might know people who can help you.

5. Alternatively look at setting yourself up in that business if that's your thing. The advice is still the same but this time you're contacting friends / family / your network for suppliers, prospects etc.

6. Believe it can happen for you. If you go in saying "why would anyone bother to take a risk on me?!?" then it will be a self-fulfilling prophecy and it will never happen for you.

In Life Reboot Camp we talk about this kind of thing a lot. In fact one of my Life Reboot Campers, Claire* signed up because she was at a bit of a loss work-wise. She had been a stay-at-home-mum for over 10 years, but her kids needed her less and she was beginning to wonder what the next step was for her. She figured out that she did want something more than being a stay at home mum, she figured out what that 'more' was and set up her own interior design company, which fits around her kids. All along the way she asked for support, advice and feedback in the private Life Reboot Camp Facebook group that accompanies the course, which meant she never felt alone as she went into this new venture.

Pretty much anything is possible when it comes to your career, as long as you are prepared to put yourself out there and go for it. You will undoubtably stumble and fall along the way, but it will be so worth it when you succeed.

* not her real name

The one with my job and sex

As an English teacher it was my job to teach my mother tongue to a variety of students. This ranged from groups of job-hunters who had their lessons paid for by the *ANPE* (job centre) to CEOs of companies, from kids playing catch-up during the school holidays to a variety of people working in tourism, and about a zillion different kinds of IT engineers.

I LOVED my job. I worked in a fun place where there was a lot of laughter and a great vibe. I met one of my best friends working there; Esta is an American who had been living in France for years, but who still got driven demented by the French as much as I did. We would share horror stories of the extreme lack of customer service in France and laugh at each other's very vulgar sense of humour. We haven't worked together since 2003, and haven't lived in the same country since 2010 but she is still one of my best friends, who still makes me laugh my arse off (or ass off as she would say).

Our boss, Françoise, was lovely, firm but fair, who also had a great sense of humour. She was French but had a great love of the English and whenever I think of her I remember her laughing.

There was a rule in the school that we would tell all students that we didn't know how to speak French, this way they HAD to speak to us in English. This was tricky for me but I quickly got used to it, and managed to get people with zero English speaking to me in the first session.

My lessons were a mix of one-to-one and group work. Sometimes I would go to a classroom the school had in the business area of Sophia Antipolis to do back-to-back lessons all day, other times they would take place in the classrooms at the language school. Several lessons and people stand out for me.

There was one man who could only take lessons in the evening after work. As I lived closest to the school and had no kids I pulled the short straw of teaching him. This meant that twice a week I would go home after a day's teaching, quickly have some dinner, then return to the school and open it back up again to teach from 8pm until 9pm.

This was a pain in the arse as I would far rather have been watching TV with my feet up, but I got paid by the hour rather than a set salary so I tended to take any hours I was offered. (I still hadn't managed to match my student temping wages with either of my French jobs, or even come close.) This man had some English already, he was what we called pre-intermediate level, so it wasn't too exhausting trying to get a conversation going. The problem was he knew enough English to be able to communicate with me, and he didn't actually want an English teacher it would seem, what he was looking for was a therapist. Lesson after lesson would go something like this:

Him "my wife, she not understand me. We have child and now me, nothing. What I do? You, you beautiful. You no have this problem."

Me: "I know! Today we are going to practise the Past Simple tense!"

From what I could tell after several attempts like this, he was feeling ignored and cast to one side by his wife, and he would very much like to know if his 23 year old English teacher would like to console him.

After a while I started to wonder how long I could keep thrusting irregular verb tables at him, before he might decide to thrust something, not related to learning English, back at me. So I ended up asking Françoise if I could swap with a male colleague, as I just didn't feel comfortable sitting in an empty building at night with this man anymore.

Next up was quite funny. I was teaching a woman who was actually pretty good at English already. She was quite an accomplished career woman from what I could tell, but possibly a little disturbed. Again she wasn't looking for an English teacher, she also wanted a therapist. Our first lesson went something like this…

"Hi! I'm Jane. I have affair with my boss, but it's ok, he leave his wife because I am *bête de sexe! Comment on dit ça en anglais?* How you say this in English? I am sex beast?!"

Taken by surprise I nodded my head, forgetting the rule that I'm not supposed to know any French.

She continued to regale me with stories of how, when and where she and her boss were having sex. Not to mention all the times she would put notes in his jacket pocket, telling him all the things she wanted to do to him, signed each time "Jane, *bête de sexe*".

I'm not sure I ever managed to complete one single lesson plan with her but her English vocabulary improved all the same. Mostly words belonging in a porn film or from the Karma Sutra, which would possibly or possibly not serve her well in her job. Either way she told me at the end of our 40 hours of lessons that I was the best English teacher ever.

After sex beast Jane it was such a come-down to teach a group of IT engineers. I quickly learned they were all the same. They'd graduated from university in 1847 and had been working at the same company ever since, and were completely incapable of using any kind of imagination.

When I taught English I would use a lot of role-play but it never worked with the IT guys.

Me: "Imagine you are in a meeting with an English man and…

Random IT geek, interrupting me: "I can no imagine".

The first few times I'd try to explain HOW they could imagine, but seeing their blank faces staring back at me I quickly gave up, and spent lessons teaching phrasal verbs, past simple tense vs present perfect tense, and reminding myself of the money this was earning me.

The last student that stands out in my mind was a male Russian ballet dancer who was performing at the Nice Opera. Françoise grabbed me before my first lesson and gushed like a teenager "he is GORGEOUS! And you've got a one-to-one lesson with him. Tell me EVERYTHING after." In all fairness I was single at the time, so she was probably delighted that she was putting such eye candy in my path.

As he walked into my classroom I could see the attraction. He had that kind of movie star chiselled face, piercing blue eyes and blond hair. But it did absolutely nothing for me. You see I have a very clear type. I go mad for Mediterranean looks, dark hair, dark eyes, that's what floats my boat. Whereas Nureyev here ticked none of those boxes. And no offence, I love a French accent, but the Russian one did nothing for me!

Unfortunately he didn't pick up on my teacher-student vibes and would sit very close to me, and tell me how beautiful I was. (Just to be clear - I am average looking, but in 1-2-1 English lessons I seemed to become a supermodel!)

One day he asked me if he could say something to me in Russian, I knew this didn't bode well so suggested he say it in English because a) he was supposed to be learning English with me and b) I don't understand any Russian. Not to be deterred he started to say something which reminded me of those war films where Russian soldiers bark harsh-sounding noises which the subtitles inform you mean "we are going to kill you all and rape your women!".

When Nureyev had finished he informed me "I just told you that you are so beautiful". It was the most I could do to hold myself back from saying "well it didn't sound like it!".

As we came out of that lesson Françoise was hovering around, ready to grin and swoon at my Russian student - it's a shame he didn't want to tell her she was beautiful, she'd have loved it! Instead he turned to me.

Nureyev: "You know, in Russia, we kiss on lips for say goodbye" as he leaned in…

Me: "Ah, well in England we don't like close contact so we shake hands" as I held out my hand and shook his.

Poor guy, I bet most other female English teachers would have been all over him, but he was just too blond and blue-eyed for me!

The one with my first French boyfriend

I might have left behind the UK and the whole adulting thing about marriage, mortgage and kids but apparently I hadn't abandoned the idea of ticking boxes to keep Society happy.

I had my degree. Tick! I had a full-time, permanent job. Tick! I looked around me - what else was on the list? Ah, a boyfriend. Hmmmmm, I was 22 but getting close to 23 and I hadn't been in a relationship since just before my 21st birthday. It was definitely time to seriously look for a boyfriend, because that was next on the list, right?

One Saturday evening Olivier, a French friend from university in the UK, got in touch to see if I wanted to go out with him, his English girlfriend and a bunch of his friends for drinks in the old town of Nice. It was a bit of a no-brainer for me as all of my friends were still working in bars, so most of my weekend evenings were spent on my own, or trying to stay awake until 2am or 3am when my friends' evenings started. Also at the time I was living opposite the bar we were to meet outside, so it literally meant just walking down the stairs to my front door and crossing the street.

The beauty of this was that my bedroom window gave me the perfect view of our meet-up point, so I waited until Olivier and his girlfriend were there before venturing down. There was quite a crowd but we had to wait before heading to a bar as Cédric hadn't turned up yet. He was pretty late and one of the girls asked "is it worth us waiting? I mean what's he like, this Cédric? Is he at least good-looking if we're waiting for him?"

Olivier, who rather fancied himself as a ladies' man, told us that Cédric wasn't too bad, but not as good-looking as him. I hadn't fallen for this 'charm' of Olivier's when we were in the UK and he tried it on with me, and decided that if Cédric was anything like him then it didn't bode well.

I consoled myself that I was out on a Saturday night, which had to be better than sitting in on my own watching shit French TV. There was alcohol and I could easily and quickly slip off and head home if it was a crap evening.

Finally Cédric turned up and he wasn't what I was expecting at all. He wasn't blond, like Olivier, so that was already a point in his favour. He was very much my type, dark hair, dark eyes, my Mediterranean type. He also wasn't full of himself like Olivier, in fact he came across as quite shy. I decided to see how the evening panned out.

We went to one of the many bars that the old town in Nice is well-known for and got drinks. In true French style this meant the guys bought half pints which they nursed for most of the night, and the girls got fruit juices, which they also dragged out for 3 hour stretches. In true Brit style I bought a pint of lager which lasted me an hour. I know it shocked most (all) of them, but I didn't care. It was Saturday night, I was young and in a bar in Nice, which was my home. I wasn't going to pretend to be someone I'm not. And let's face it a pint an hour for a 20-something Brit is NOTHING!

After an hour or so I ended up sitting next to Cédric and decided to spark up a conversation with him. He seemed like a nice enough guy, he was physically attractive, didn't seem like a dick, was single apparently, not 100 years old, and I had decided it was time for me to tick the next box on my list - get a boyfriend.

The conversation was stilted. Not from my lack of French for once. It was just a bit awkward. I definitely shocked him with my beer drinking, and he was certainly a quiet, shy guy, so quite the opposite to this loud-mouthed, extrovert girl. We did talk though and I found out that he was working with Olivier, temporarily, at Europcar at the airport. That made sense as they definitely didn't seem like people who would be friends normally.

By about midnight everyone was beginning to talk about heading home (shocking for France as night clubs don't open until gone 11pm) so we started to say goodbye to each other. This kind of thing takes a looooooooong time as you have to go round everyone giving two kisses (one on each cheek) and say things like "it was lovely to meet you, have a good evening / night", even if you haven't said two words to each other since doing all the kissing stuff at the start of the evening. (At least it's only 2 kisses in Nice, in other parts of France it's 3 or even 4 kisses each time!)

I didn't have the courage to ask for Cédric's phone number but I did think he was boyfriend material so resolved to ask Olivier for it afterwards.

Later on that week I did just that and found myself speaking to Cédric's mum on the phone, asking if he was home. This was back in the days before mobile phones were a common thing and you had to ring people on their landline, and run the risk of getting someone's parent at the other end. Yikes!

Cédric seemed mildly surprised that I had got his number and called him; after a bit of small talk I asked him if he wanted to go out for a drink one evening, and we fixed a date for a few days later. I was excited at the prospect of a boyfriend, it had been a while and I was feeling lonely with all my friends working opposite hours to me.

Our first date was more promising than the night we met. Cédric seemed more relaxed and the conversation flowed a lot more smoothly this time round. We even had our first kiss! YES! I was well on my way to ticking that box.

Little by little our relationship progressed and we officially became boyfriend and girlfriend. I told my parents about him, he met my flatmates and friends, and about 6 weeks later he invited me up to the local ski resort on new year's day to spend a couple of nights there with his friends.

I was nervous about going, I only knew one couple who were going and the girl seemed to HATE me. On top of that I had only 'skied' once before, when living in Nice as a student, it was a disaster, and scared the crap out of me, causing me to swear off skiing for the rest of my life.

I arrived at the apartment in the mountains with sweaty palms and a full on party of butterflies in my belly. What if that girl was a bitch to me? I was stuck in the mountains now for a couple of nights. What if I attempted to ski and humiliated myself? Or broke something?

Cédric welcomed me into the apartment with a big grin on his face and introduced me to the other couple, Gilles and Sandra, who were just the loveliest people, and who totally made up for Céline who definitely hated me. Every time she looked at me it was like she was sucking on a lemon. I just wasn't sure what I'd done to piss her off, I'd barely spoken 10 words to her in the whole time I'd known her.

I shrugged it off as I watched her be a cow to her boyfriend, maybe this was just who she was. But that first night as we converted sofas into double beds and all got ready to hit the sack, she went crazy. Raging at her boyfriend and just acting like she should be locked up. It was only once everyone was safely tucked away in their cubby holes of the apartment that I asked Cédric in a whisper what the hell was going on.

It turned out that she was in love with Cédric, despite being in a long-term relationship with his oldest and best friend (and neighbour), and didn't appreciate the fact that Cédric kept turning her down. Now with the arrival of a girlfriend on the scene (me) it was looking less and less likely that Cédric would screw his friend over, and get together with Céline. Hence her hatred for me.

I was discovering a whole new France to the "*Monsieur Dupont est boulanger*" that I had learnt at school. As I met more of Cédric's friends it seemed that French women were deranged in general when it came to men. (I did meet some 'normal' and lovely French women later on.)

A few weeks later Cédric and I were out in Nice where we were meeting another of his best friends, Edouard, and his girlfriend, Sylvie. Let me give you some background before I explain what happened next. At this stage I was 22, Cédric was 27, Sylvie was 25 and Edouard was 40 (i.e. about 100 years old in my eyes). He was also a father; he had a 15 year old daughter with one ex-girlfriend, and a 5 year old daughter with another ex. Edouard and Sylvie had not been together long and he had been in a relationship when they got together.

So back to our meeting in a bar / nightclub in Nice. It was a Saturday night so naturally I was dressed up for a night out, quite conservatively for a 20-something Brit I have to say. I was wearing a nice pair of trousers and fitted top. Not tight trousers, not a tight top. No cleavage on display. No crop tops. No mini skirts. No legs on display. No boobs on display. No excessive make-up. As I say, it was pretty conservative.

As Cédric introduced me to Edouard and Sylvie she literally threw her arms around his neck, so that as we leaned in to give each other the standard two hello kisses she was clinging to him and showing her possession of him. It was hilarious to observe. Almost primal, I'm surprised she didn't piss on him. I really wanted to laugh and say "I'm here with my new boyfriend, I am sooooo not interested in your relic of a boyfriend, so don't worry love!" But I didn't, I just smiled and kissed her frosty cheeks.

My relationship with Cédric was the first time I'd really got to see French people, society and culture up close and it really was fascinating just how different it was from what I knew in the UK, and what I'd learnt at university. Even though I'd lived in France as a student and had 'seen' a French guy for a month or so whilst there, this was all so new.

During my relationship with Cédric I got the impression there was little to no sisterhood in France. I also found relationships quite different in France to in the UK. Over my years there every relationship that I knew of broke down when one party left for someone else. They never came to an end because the couple got bored of each other, or the arguments were too much, there was always someone else involved on one side or another. Which gave me the impression that there wasn't much trust in relationships. I also noticed that French men rarely went out without their girlfriends, and most French women didn't seem to trust other females with their boyfriends.

I never slipped into this lack of trust of Cédric. He was a good guy, not a cheater at all, we were happy enough, why would I even question him? Maybe if I had been more 'French' or more suspicious what happened later on would have gone down very differently…

Task - how to stop ticking boxes

We do a lot of things in life because we are ticking boxes that Society, parents, teachers or others put in front of us. Those studies. That university. That job. That house. That area. That relationship. Getting married. Having kids. What school the kids go to and so on, from birth through to death.

But let me share a game-changer with you - you don't have to tick other people's boxes. You can do pretty much what you want, as long as it's legal. It's preferable if it's moral too and doesn't hurt others.

Don't get me wrong, Cédric is the loveliest guy and I had some really nice times with him, but I would never have even considered a relationship with him if I hadn't had Society's boxes to be ticked burnt into my brain. Which included the idea that it was time for me to be in a relationship and to settle down.

Maybe you are a people-pleaser, maybe you don't like to break rules. But let me ask you this - on your deathbed are you going to regret not letting yourself be happy, or are you going to feel relieved that you kept people happy?

Right here and right now I give you permission to be happy. Because do you know what? Anyone who loves you wants you to be happy. If they don't that is a clear sign that they don't love you.

Which means it's important that you figure out what makes you happy.

Don't enter into jobs, relationships, house moves, marriages, babies or anything else unless it is the right thing for you, and is not just because you are people-pleasing, or doing what you 'should' do or what Society expects of you.

Screw Society and everyone else! They're not living your life day in, day out.

Next time you are getting into something new - a job, relationship, house, decision - and it doesn't quite feel right you need to ask yourself if you're just doing it to tick boxes.

That job with a great title, corner office and big old pay packet, but with dubious practices. Do you really want to do that work or do you just want to share that you're climbing the career ladder, like a good girl is supposed to?

That relationship with a guy who is nice, and that your whole family loves, but where there is no fire, passion, excitement or proper love. Is that what you want? Do you want to just be content or bursting with happiness? (Don't get me wrong, I don't think anyone is happy all day, every day, but I do believe in feeling happy every day, at least once.)

That house with the price tag that makes you scared, that doesn't really feel like a home. Is it for you? Or for other people? To make your parents happy? To impress your friends? To tick another box for others?

Every time something feels off, wrong, icky or doesn't sit well with you take a moment to ask yourself if it's what YOU really want, or if you're just ticking boxes for others.

Take a moment now to list all the big things going on in your life and ask yourself "does this make me happy or am I ticking boxes?". For example:

- Your relationship
- Your home
- Your job
- Your kids' school
- Your kids' activities
- Your hobbies
- Your clothes

To make doing this book's tasks easier head to www.SophieLeBrozec.com/happy-bonus and download all the tasks in one PDF that is easy to print and easy to go through (along with other bonuses including the audio version of this book, a checklist of how to be happy and a motivational kick up the bum audio).

The one where I was cheated on and dumped

Like lots of relationships where things go wrong, I thought we were doing fine, but with hindsight I realised we were stuck in a rut. We were going about our lives, in our little routine, but our relationship was totally stagnant. I believed - at the time - that this was what a grown-up relationship looked like. I thought that the crazy, fireworks love was what happened when you were 17 and it was your first love, when your emotions are so raw you feel like you need to vomit or cry from the intensity of it all. I didn't realise you could have that same kind of love once you were an adult. I (wrongly) assumed that adult love and adult relationships were about going to DIY shops and supermarkets on a Saturday, watching TV in silence, getting things done on the to do list, and not having fun. How wrong I was.

We were comfortable, we were friendly, we got on well. We never argued. Every meal was eaten in front of the TV, usually the news. We talked a bit about our respective days at work as we prepared the evening meal, companionably, but that was it. We were like flatmates who had become friends, and who ran a pretty good ship together. We were not what I thought we were - two people in love, in a grown-up relationship.

But I was ticking my boxes. We'd bought a house together - tick. We'd been together for two and a half years (serious relationship) - tick. His parents and his family were like my adopted family in France, and my parents got on well with all of them too. It felt like it was only a matter of time before I fulfilled the inevitable that I had cited to everyone before leaving the UK - marriage, mortgage and kids.

I wasn't sad but I wasn't happy either. I was just living, on this kind of an even keel. There were things to be done, I did them. Go to work, do grocery shopping, cook dinner, clear up from dinner, clean the house, pay the bills, fill in my tax return and so on and so forth. I truly believed this was adult life. The incredible highs of my teens and early twenties were part of the past. I believed grown-ups keep things steady, there is very little - to no - raucous laughter, there is no being silly, there are jobs to be done, tasks to be completed, chores to be got through. There was no time for laughter and fun in all that. You did what you needed to do and then collapsed in front of the TV, before falling asleep and doing it all over again the next day.

I honestly didn't know that my life could be fun, full of laughter, that I could feel happiness, excitement, that I could be silly no matter my age, that it was up to me to choose the emotions and feelings I wanted in my life. I didn't know all that. And Cédric and I were in a rut. There was no love, and certainly no fireworks.

But that didn't stop me from being hurt so badly by what happened next.

I remember it so clearly. It was the day before Fathers Day 2001, we had just collected my parents at the airport and were taking them home. It was late, nearly midnight, but we didn't have much petrol in the car, so Cédric suggested that he drop us home before going off to fill the car up. It made complete sense as we were heading off quite early the next day to have a two family Fathers Day - his parents, siblings and their families + my parents and my brother, Tim, who was living in Nice at the time.

Everything seemed completely normal as I dropped off to sleep, little did I know the bombshell that awaited me the next day.

We woke up on Fathers Day morning and were in bed talking about the logistics for the day ahead. I needed to give Tim a quick call so I asked Cédric for his phone; at that time certain mobile phone operators gave free / cheaper calls to phone numbers in the same network, so we used to use my phone to call certain people and Cédric's phone to call others. And we always called Tim from Cédric's phone. In fact we had called him from the airport the night before at 10pm, so I just hit last number redial, and my heart stopped.

Because it wasn't Tim's number at 10pm that came up. The screen read "Sabine" and the call was made around midnight.

A bit of background to fill you in on why this made my heart stop. Sabine was one of Cédric's colleagues, she'd started at his company about 6 months previously and, based on what I had already seen of French women and what Cédric had told me about the things she said and did at work, I KNEW she wanted him. But I hadn't said anything as I totally trusted Cédric, and didn't want to be a mad jealous Frenchwoman like those I'd witnessed over the previous few years. However it would appear that my fears had some roots.

I called Tim, somehow managing to keep my voice calm and normal, then turned to Cédric and asked him:

"Is it normal to call your female colleague on a Saturday night at midnight? Was there some kind of work emergency I didn't know about?" in a voice leaden with sarcasm.

What I didn't expect was Cédric's super defensive response of "don't blame me! You must know that our relationship hasn't been great recently!"

Our 'conversation' had to be cut short as we were running late for our big Fathers Day picnic, but my stomach was a knot of nerves, my mind was running numerous movie tracks, none of which made me feel good, and the tears kept threatening to spill. I gave myself a pep talk; my parents were there, I was SO happy to see them and I didn't want to ruin our time together or have them worry about me. I planted a big smile on my face as I asked them how they'd slept.

I refused breakfast as I knew nothing would get past the great big ball in my throat. At the picnic I couldn't eat either, the fact that Sabine was skinny (in fact I was pretty certain she was anorexic) meant I started to berate myself for being a big, fat pig and scaring my man off into the arms of a better woman. Just to be clear, I was a UK size 10 (US size 6) at the time, so definitely no fatty.

I could see my mum looking at me strangely, and I knew I would have to eat soon as I would never convince her I was ok otherwise. I love my mum to bits and she knows me so well, including just how much I love my food!

After the picnic lunch Cédric and I managed to excuse ourselves to go for a walk, leaving everyone chilling and chatting. I remember it like it was yesterday, we were in these woods and there was a great big electric pylon in amongst the trees. I asked him what was going on with Sabine and he tried to tell me that nothing had happened between them (the 'yet' hung unspoken in the air). But that he was attracted to her and she was attracted to him. Although of course in true French style she was in a relationship with another guy, and was living with him too. Because why on earth would you leave someone if you don't have another relationship to step right into?!

I asked him how, why, what had I done? He told me it wasn't about me, but it was about both of us, that we'd never had that lightning bolt of love, never had any kind of fireworks. It had always just been very comfortable. At the time I really didn't want to hear it. This was my next box ticking - surely we were going to get married and have 2.4 children? Him falling in love with his colleague and leaving me totally wasn't in my plan.

With hindsight I can say I totally agree with him. We shouldn't have been together, there was no real love there, there was compassion and friendship but nothing of true love or a true relationship. I couldn't see it at the time though. I was humiliated. My dreams were coming crashing down. What next? I finally found myself asking.

He didn't know. He didn't want to hurt me but he also wanted to know whether he should be exploring a relationship with Sabine. I suddenly realised that in less than 2 months we had a flight booked back to the UK for my sister's wedding. She was the first of our generation getting married and it was a big deal. I asked him if we could still go to the UK and go to the wedding together, and then he could do what he wanted after. I didn't want my big break-up news to take the spotlight off my sister on her big day.

He agreed and we settled into an uncomfortable existence. We carried on as before but there was a big old elephant following us around every room we were in. We no longer borrowed each other's phones to make calls and his phone suddenly developed a code overnight that I didn't know. Yes, I did try to access it once when he was in the shower, which I think makes me entirely human.

We didn't mention what was going on to anyone. I think he felt too bad about what he was doing, and I was too humiliated. I was also desperately hoping this would all blow over, we'd go back to normal, and I didn't want anyone knowing about that piece of dirty laundry, thank you very much.

If people asked me why I was getting skinnier and skinnier, I didn't mention that I was trying to compete with my boyfriend's affections with an anorexic, nor that I struggled to swallow any morsels of food. My hips jutted out further, my already slim stomach became concave, my regular clothes hung off me and I compared myself incessantly to the uber-skinny blond he worked with day in, day out, hoping that this skinnier version of me might stand more of a chance against her.

D-Day came around and we flew to the UK for my sister's wedding. It was a wonderful day and I drew on the love of my family as the sun shone down on us. At one point my sister - completely ignorant to what was going on in my relationship - tried to set me up with one of her colleagues, who was very good-looking and completely my type. Maybe she had some kind of sixth sense that I needed the boost as he chatted me up.

The hardest thing was trying to make sure that Cédric didn't appear on any official wedding photos. That and trying not to burst into tears every time someone smiled and said "it'll be you two next!". A couple of times I was tempted to blurt out "no it won't because we're splitting up when we get back to France!" but I managed to just smile and change the subject.

We arrived back in France as summer was coming to an end, it was time for *La Rentrée* (when kids and the whole country goes back to school and work) and there was a sense of change in the air. Except *chez nous* where absolutely no change was happening. We were still cohabiting each room with an elephant, with neither of us mentioning 'the situation'.

Eventually I couldn't take it anymore and asked him what was going on, to which he burst into tears (for the first time ever in our relationship) and cried onto my shoulder that he was so lost and didn't know what to do. I really wanted to tell him that obviously the right decision was staying with me and telling the anorexic to take a hike. But the sensible realist in me told him that he had to choose one way or the other, because it wasn't good for anyone, even though I knew I might lose him forever. Which is exactly what happened.

He picked her not me. Just the knowledge hit me like a bowling ball in the gut. He picked her not me. I was not worthy. I wasn't skinny enough. I wasn't blond enough. I wasn't French enough. Maybe I should have held in my Sophie-ness even more, my swearing, my burps, my farts. I mean I did conceal them massively, but I should have done more. I should have conformed more and I wouldn't have lost him. I was convinced this was all my fault. I wasn't good enough and now I would be left on the shelf forever at the age of 25.

I also thought it was that anorexic cow's fault too (as I began to refer to her in my head), she had hunted down a perfectly good man, in a perfectly good relationship, with absolutely no thought for her fellow woman. No thought for sisterhood! I ranted and railed about her at the time. But I never blamed him.

I hit rock bottom and convinced myself I was worthless. There was even one scary fleeting moment where I even questioned carrying on. Fortunately it didn't last long and was the impetus to start really living again.

By the time I began telling people, I had more or less come to terms with it all. I was still gutted and humiliated, but not so angry anymore. I remember a close friend, who knew both Cédric and I very well, telling me to go to his office, punch her in the face, and tell her he was my man and to keep her hands off! She then proceeded to tell me I should try and get pregnant, to force him to pick me (truly scary the way some people's minds work). At the time I was listening to George Michael on repeat, well one song of his "I can't make you love me", and I told her "I don't want to force him to be with me, I want him to want to be with me. I can't make him love me."

Cédric and I discussed the logistics of our break-up - luckily there was little paperwork, no kids, no divorce. But there was a house, its furnishings and our two cats. I told him he could take anything as long as I got to keep both cats. He was incredibly generous and let me keep most things, and just asked that I pay him back the deposit he put down on the house so that I could keep my home and stay living there.

I am incredibly lucky that a) my parents and one of my sisters agreed to lend me money so that I could pay Cédric back and keep the house (I sold it 2 years later, made a great profit and paid them back with interest), and b) that we had bought it for a pittance so I was able to extend the mortgage by 10 years and afford the monthly payments on my meagre salary. At the time I was only earning 5,000 francs (approximately $833) some months, as I was still on my hourly teaching pay, which wouldn't have got me far on the French Riviera!

When we said goodbye there was no animosity. We didn't argue once in the whole relationship or subsequent break-up, and to this day I wish him well. Because if he had not had the balls to end that relationship, which was going nowhere, and wasn't a good relationship at all, then I would not have known the exquisite and intense happiness and pleasure I have had since, when I met the love of my life, Ben.

Task - how to deal with rock bottom

It feels like the end of the world. It doesn't matter if your rock bottom is due to a relationship, your work, your finances, your living arrangements or anything else, the feeling is the same. Like you're at the bottom of a well or a pit, and you can't get out. It feels like things will never be ok again. Like you will never smile or be happy again. It can feel like trying to get through everyday life is a mountain that you are not equipped to climb.

If you are feeling this way I want you to know that things can and do get better. Your world has been rocked and will never be the same again, but that's good because it means it could be even better than before. You might not be able to envisage HOW but believe me, if you can hold on to the idea that it can and will get better you're already a good way down that path.

Don't cling to what was. That has gone. Things are different now. What can you learn from this? What will you do differently next time? How can you get the best out of this situation for you moving forwards?

Don't try and plan what you're going to do next month. Don't try and figure out who you're going to take to the family summer barbecue. Don't attempt to work out where you'll be work-wise in one year. Concentrate on today. And if that's too much, concentrate on right now. What are you going to do for the next 5 minutes? Little by little you will build this up, and you will be able to plan ahead again. But for now, concentrate on getting through one day, one morning, one hour at a time.

What one thing can you do that's a step in the right direction? Have a shower? Cook some dinner? See a friend for a coffee? Update your CV? Go for a walk? What are you capable of right now?

I love Steve Jobs' speech about connecting the dots:

"Again, you can't connect the dots looking forward; you can only connect them looking backward. So you have to trust that the dots will somehow connect in your future. You have to trust in something — your gut, destiny, life, karma, whatever. This approach has never let me down, and it has made all the difference in my life."

I hadn't heard this idea when I hit my first rock bottom after Cédric left me, but somehow I found this in me. I believed that this would all work out in the end, and I would understand WHY looking back. So I kept just going through my life, one day at a time, one foot in front of the other, believing that things would get better.

Other things that have helped me when I've been at rock bottom which you might like to try out are:

- Gratitude. When life just doesn't feel bearable, when I feel like I've been dealt the worst hand ever, I use gratitude to flip my mindset on it all. No matter how awful things seem there is always something to be grateful for - a roof over your head, food in the cupboard, people who love you, your health, a job to provide you with financial security. The good thing about gratitude is the more you practise it the more good stuff comes your way :-)

- Journalling. Writing down all the crap stuff that is whirring around in my head, getting it out onto paper actually reduces the fear and anxiety of it all. Scribbling down your worst fears is a bit like switching the light on and seeing there is no monster under the bed.

- Visualising. You can keep playing over the awful moment when your partner left you, when you got fired, when you realised you'd lost a ton of money or whatever it was that pushed you to rock bottom. But that shit will just keep you on a downward spiral. If you want to find your way out of the dark hole you're in (which I'm guessing you do, as otherwise why are you reading this book?!?) then you need to change the movie reel. What do you WANT? What partner / relationship, what job / career / business, what home, what life? Spend your time thinking about and picturing that rather than replaying the bad stuff that happened to you. Even though that is easier. It's comforting in a screwed up way. But to move onwards and upwards you need to change things. Remember what the very wise Rumi said when you feel like you can't bear this pain and suffering:

"The wound is the place where the Light enters you."
— Rumi

You will learn so much from this bad time. You will be better, stronger, happier for it. You probably can't see it, feel it or imagine it now but this will likely turn out to be a good thing for you in the end. Even if only to write in a book to teach others ;-)

One of the things that got me through this period of my life when Cédric left me and I hit rock bottom is called "woo-woo", although I didn't know what it was called at the time. I was using my mind to dictate and control my life and my future. Since then, by accident or intentionally, I have moulded my life according to what I want. Jobs and businesses I love, houses and people that have shown up in my life, and even my incredible house move and new dream life here in Mauritius. I'm so into it that the whole of Module 2 of Life Reboot Camp is entitled "Woo-woo" and is dedicated to getting what you want out of life.

If you are at rock bottom or need help feeling better or more upbeat in general then grab my free book bonuses; the checklist to feel happy and the 'kick up the rear' audio should both really help you, and you can refer to them whenever you need them. Download them here: www.SophieLeBrozec.com/happy-bonus

The one where I met my husband in a bar

I'm not going to lie, that whole period with Cédric was a dark, dark time for me. There were parts of me that came to the surface that I'd never seen before. I've nearly always been a strong person, full of self-confidence, self-worth and self-esteem, but this rejection knocked me for six. And it's not even because I felt like Cédric was the love of my life and I couldn't live without him. I'd known from early on that this wasn't some great love.

I remember this hitting me so clearly one day in July 2000. My parents were over visiting us in France and we were having sundowners on the beach with them. After the sun had set and the stars had come out they wandered down the beach, hand-in-hand, chatting and laughing, and looking just like an advert for what a couple in love looked like. But they weren't in the throes of new love; at that stage they had been married for over 30 years and had had 5 children together. As I watched them act like newlyweds I thought about my own relationship, and realised that we were only a year and a half into it yet we weren't like that. In fact we had never been like that.

So even a year before the infamous Fathers Day I knew we didn't have *that* kind of relationship, the one I'd always hoped I'd have. One like my parents' relationship. Yet I was still devastated when Cédric's bombshell hit. Because I was giving up on my dream. I was in love with his family, who had taken me in like their own. I was in love with the future I thought we had in store; he was a good, stable guy and I was certain he'd be a good dad (I also thought he'd be a good, loyal husband! Ha!). That was what I was mourning.

Also I'd never lived alone. I'd gone from my parents' house to house-sharing at university, to apartment-sharing in Nice, to living with Cédric. Could I live alone?

On top of all that was the crushing humiliation. Not only was our relationship over, but it was over because he was leaving me for a skinny blond. It was a total rejection of me, of my curves, of who I am. To the extent that - along with the not-eating and losing tons of weight - I also considered dying my hair blond.

Yes, it would appear all rational thinking goes out of the window when you are rejected and hurt emotionally.

To get through my days in the aftermath of Cédric moving out I would repeat to myself over and over "there is someone out there for you who is far better than Cédric, he loves you to the moon and back and treats you like you deserve to be treated, and the feeling is mutual, it is the most incredible relationship" or words to that effect. I didn't have them written down I just kept repeating this general idea.

Funnily enough I never said or thought about who this guy would be, what he would look like, any of his attributes, how I would meet him or anything like that. I just held strong to the idea that he was out there and we were going to find each other.

At this stage I had never heard of the law of attraction or manifesting - this idea that through your mind, your thoughts, your beliefs, your feelings you have control over what happens in your life. I'd never heard of it yet I was practising it without realising it, and it didn't take long for my 'mantra' to come true for me.

My friends were great and would invite me out all the time so I didn't have to feel alone and lonely, and I said yes to every invitation. I remember one night in particular, as it was the first time I kissed a guy after Cédric. It was Hallowe'en, about a month and a half after Cédric and I officially split up, and we were out in Nice, I was dressed as a red devil and this younger guy had been chatting me up. Egged on by my friends I ended up kissing him at the end of the night….and promptly burst into tears. It felt wrong. It felt like I was cheating on Cédric. I wasn't ready to move on it would seem.

But as I repeated my 'mantra' every day, and kept living my life in the day to day, things got easier. I went out each weekend and found myself getting asked for my phone number as my vibe changed. I was no longer giving out 'attached girl' vibes or 'victim' vibes. I was giving out 'I'm getting on with my life and am happy' vibes and apparently this attracted guys.

I enjoyed this attention but decided I didn't want a relationship just yet. I was exhausted with what had happened with Cédric, and I just wanted to be, and to live for a while. That was until 1st December 2001 when everything changed.

I'd been out shopping that day and had bought a nice top and trousers; I had very little money but by shopping in the cheaper shops I managed to make myself feel better without my overdraft going into free-fall. I also still wasn't spending much on food. Neither of which is necessarily a recommendation. It's just how I got through this trying time.

Despite it being Nice and the French Riviera it was still cold. It was December after all. And I didn't feel like going out. But my best friend Nikki, another English expat, rang me up and begged me. She was after this guy, Paolo, who worked in *Pompei* bar in Nice; they'd got together a couple of times and she didn't want to drop off his radar. I didn't feel like going out but I had new clothes that were crying to be worn, and my alternative was dinner in front of the TV by myself. So I gave in, got my glad rags on and headed out.

Little did I know that a few towns away was a guy, who also wanted to stay at home that night, but his friend Laurent was down in Nice from Paris for the weekend, so he felt obligated to go out and see him.

Nikki and I rocked up at *Pompei* and immediately said hi to Paolo, asking him if he could find us somewhere to sit. We had coats with us and didn't want to be stood holding them all night (*Pompei* isn't the kind of classy establishment with cloakrooms for coats). But it was busy and there were no free tables. Paolo, clearly liking the attention he was getting from Nikki, tried to find a solution for us. There were two guys sitting opposite each other at a table with two spare seats, Paolo told us to wait as he would see if we could sit with them.

He came back with a smile on his face; we could have the seats as long as we vacated them when these guys' friends arrived. Nikki and I sat down, across the table from each other, next to these guys. We smiled tight 'I don't know you' polite smiles as we said *bonsoir*. Then we proceeded to dissect Paolo's behaviour and words since we arrived, chatting away in English together. Did he seem keen? Might they hook up later? How should Nikki play it?

After a while we were both merry with a few drinks inside us and Nikki had to go to the toilet. As this was back in the days when a mobile phone was a fairly boring device I didn't pull my phone out. Instead I slid closer to these two strange guys who we'd been sharing a table with and (slightly drunkenly) said to them in French "I'm sorry about us speaking in English, I hope you don't find it rude but we're both English and it would be weird to chat in French". I only said it as I was bored, waiting for Nikki while she was in the loo.

The guys grinned back that it was fine as they both understood English and so it didn't bother them. Oh crap! I thought. Had we talked about them at all?? I couldn't think of anything so carried on chatting to them. Random, semi-drunk, Saturday night chat to strangers in bars - what's your name, what do you do, how old are you etc. It turned out they were twins, which I got them to prove by showing me ID (I also wanted to check out their ages, having been chatted up recently by a 19 year old. The shame of it!). They looked young but were in fact just a few weeks younger than me. Right I could carry on chatting. I still wasn't looking for a relationship but this was fun.

Nikki came back from the toilet and caught me mid-chat with these two guys, so joined in but dropped them like a hot potato whenever Paolo came nearby. She really was hooked on him. Because I wasn't looking for a relationship, or looking to impress, I talked absolute shite to these poor buggers. I was still pissed off with the lack of sisterhood amongst French women so I was on a bit of a French women bash. I went on about French women being all prim and proper, and pretending they were perfect when everyone knows they burp and fart just like every other human. At their shocked faces I told them a secret "you do realise that even the queen of England burps, farts and shits like everyone else, don't you?". They were quite unused to anyone like me, who wasn't trying to act perfectly to chat them up, who was just being completely herself and natural, and saying it like it was.

Because I didn't care about the outcome of this evening I said whatever I was thinking, it was completely uncensored and we ended up laughing. A lot. Their friends came, but by that stage we were nicely ensconced in their seats, so they ended up having to stand.

By the end of the night I realised I'd had the most fun I'd had in a LONG time and I didn't want it to end. The one I'd been sitting next to, the one I'd chatted to the most, and the one I'd clicked with the most - Ben - asked me for my phone number, which I happily gave to him. This time really hoping that he would call me. I still didn't want a relationship, but I'd had so much fun with him that I wanted to see him again, and saw us becoming good friends. Even if he was yet another IT engineer, like the awful imagination-less grey men I taught English too. But he didn't seem like he was cut from the same cloth.

We parted ways and after he left I tried to remember what he looked like, but I couldn't. It had been dark in the bar, I had been merry (not full on drunk) and as we were sat next to each other I didn't get a good look at him. I just remembered that he had dark hair and dark eyes - tick and tick - and that I'd felt a real connection with him.

On the Sunday I felt good and wasn't at all worried that I didn't hear from him. I was only interested in him as a friend so that was fine. On the Monday I got a text message mid-morning as I switched on my phone in between two English lessons, it said (in French) "It's not nice of me to disturb a teacher while she's working…". I grinned and quickly fired off a reply.

We ping-ponged text messages to and fro all day. Messages of everything and nothing. That evening we then sent each other longer messages via email, once we got home to our respective computers. By the Tuesday we were talking about meeting up but we both had lots going on that week, and he was going to Avignon the weekend after, where he was from and where his parents still lived.

On the Wednesday evening I was going rollerblading in Nice and he was going to be in a bar with his friends, right by where I'd be when I finished. I agreed to pop in for one drink afterwards at about 10pm. Famous last words.

I worried about whether I would recognise him (this was way before the days of social media) but as we saw each other on the street outside the bar, I knew it was him, without a shadow of a doubt. And thought to myself "hmmmm, not only is he a lovely guy that you click with but he's also very good-looking!".

We walked into the bar together where I was met with 6 of his male friends sitting at a round table, all looking up at me. Yikes! But I quickly remembered I had nothing to prove, I wasn't looking for a relationship, and they could take me or leave me. Ben and I chatted endlessly, and from time to time friends of his would chat to me too. When I was putting off going home, even though it was 2am and the bar was emptying out, I started to admit to myself that these were not just friendly feelings I had for him. Especially when one of his friends, Hervé, asked me for my phone number. In front of Ben. Which felt a bit weird. I mean, I knew I didn't want a relationship, but I'd never said that to him, so this felt a bit strange. I shrugged it off, not knowing that the next day all would become clear…

I got home shortly before 3am (when I had to be up at 6.30am for work - teaching my boss's husband English, gulp!) and realised that I had more feelings for this guy than I'd been willing to admit. Hervé asking for my phone number had made me realise that I wasn't interested in anyone else, and that I *was* interested in Ben.

High on the evening's euphoria of chatting, bonding and clicking with this man who was feeling a lot less like a stranger, I sent him a text message asking if we could meet for a drink after work the next day (Thursday). I was supposed to be having dinner at Cédric's friends' house (you remember Edouard and Sylvie who I couldn't stand? Well that's how desperate I was in my "say yes to every invitation"!), but I couldn't wait until after the weekend to see Ben again, so wanted to squeeze in a quick drink before going to theirs.

We met at a bar / restaurant in the business area of Sophia Antipolis called Le Montparnasse. It was pretty quiet as this area is mostly surrounded by offices, so it is packed at lunchtime but quiet afterwards because, as we already know, the French don't do after work drinks like the Brits do!

Yet again we slipped into easy banter, chatting on and on, barely coming up for breath. 1 hour passed in 1 second and Ben asked me if I could change my plans so we could have dinner together there. It took me a nano-second to decide that ditching Edouard and Sylvie was the right thing to do, I called them and settled in for an evening with Ben.

We laughed and joked. It was flirtatious. It was exciting. I knew I wanted more than just friendship from this man. There was something there. I knew I'd said I didn't want a relationship, but I couldn't even put into words what was going on here. If I knew more about this kind of stuff I'd say that we had known each other in a past life, we were that comfortable in each other's company from the get-go.

In what felt like 5 minutes it was 11.30pm and we were being kicked out of the restaurant. Without realising it, we had been the last ones there for a long time. Despite 3 hours sleep the night before, followed by a long day of teaching I was buzzing. I hadn't felt so alive in such a long time.

As Ben and I dawdled back to the car park, both of us seeming to want to make the time last longer, we talked some more. About anything and everything. We stopped to say goodbye as we got to our respective cars. But instead of the standard kiss on each cheek Ben lent in and gave me the most incredible kiss on the mouth. It was electric and exciting, but at the same time felt familiar and comforting. It's a shame that what came next was so shocking.

Almost immediately he pulled away and told me

"I'm not a nice guy because I'm not single".

I couldn't believe it. After everything that had gone on with Cédric, and me ranting on about French women going after other women's boyfriends, here I was doing - accidentally - the exact same thing. But suddenly I was the scarlet woman.

I was devastated. What I felt with Ben was like nothing I'd ever felt before. How could I have been so wrong? And what now? I'd just come from months of Cédric's indecision over two women, and I really wasn't ready to go through that again.

"I don't like ultimatums but I don't share and I think there is too much between us to just be friends, so it's up to you now…" I told him.

I was so proud of myself. I really liked this guy, but I was beginning to build my self-esteem up again and I wasn't prepared to let it get wrecked by a man again.

I asked Ben how serious it was and he told me they'd been together 6 months but he'd known her for years and that it was a long distance relationship. This was why he was going away for the weekend, to see her at his mum's house in Avignon.

I felt sick. What chance did I have? I was obviously just a bit of fun whilst he was away from his girlfriend. But at least it made Hervé's behaviour the night before understandable, as far as he was concerned I was fair game as Ben was already spoken for. Ben managed to convince me to meet him for lunch the next day, before he headed off after work to see his girlfriend.

He picked me up in his car at lunchtime and as I got into his car I heard a song playing that I was obsessed with at the time "*Le vent emportera*" by *Noir Désir*. This made me smile as we had already had a conversation about music tastes which went a bit like this:

Ben "what kind of music do you like?"

Me "pretty much anything really."

Ben "well there must be some music you don't like?"

Me "no, not really, well except heavy metal of course, but then NOBODY likes heavy metal!"

About an hour later

Me "you never told me what kind of music you like"

Ben "heavy metal"

Me "mwahahahaha! You're just saying that as I said I hate heavy metal"

Ben "no, I really love heavy metal"

Me "oh"

So to get into his car, for the first song we should listen to together, chosen by him and not just randomly on the radio, to be a song I couldn't get enough of at the time. For me it was a sign that this was something special.

I'd barely buckled my seatbelt before I blurted out "so, have you made a decision yet?". Cool Sophic, so cool, no neediness at all! But I didn't have to worry, as we drove to the restaurant he proceeded to tell me that he was going to drive to Avignon that evening and tell his girlfriend that it was over. Just like that.

Cédric had spent months crying on my shoulder, telling me he was lost and didn't know what to do, until I finally told him to make a decision, one way or the other. And here was Ben, cool as you like, telling me he was going to end his relationship less than a week after he'd met me. Just one day after he'd kissed me for the first time. Easy as can be.

I have to say that it gave me so much respect for him. He didn't want to mess either of us around and, as he told me, if he had these kinds of feelings for me after less than a week then it clearly meant his relationship had no future, whether he and I worked out or not.

I spent the whole lunch with the biggest love-sick teenage grin on my face. When it was time to say goodbye I felt sick though. What if he saw his girlfriend and he changed his mind? Or she convinced him to stay? I couldn't eat all weekend and was severely restless but I didn't dare message him or call him. I tried to keep busy but my mind kept going to the worst case scenario.

I planned my favourite yummy dinner, *Tartiflette*, for him for the Sunday evening, a kind of a 'you made the right decision' prize. I waited for news, and waited. Finally late Sunday afternoon I got a brief text "I'm leaving now, I'll call you when I'm back".

What did that mean? Did that mean he hadn't split up with her? Or he had? Or he hadn't? Or what? Cue more tummy flip flops. Finally my phone rang, the caller ID revealing it was Ben. I tried to act all cool and undemanding but within about 2 seconds I had already asked him what happened, to which I got the answer I'd been waiting for: it's over.

We arranged for him to come straight over so we could have dinner and chat, as two young, free, single 20-somethings. I am pleased to say he was very impressed by this Brit gal's ability to cook a yummy French dish. And before I knew it we had talked until gone midnight.

I was flying high. In seventh heaven. I was being ME and this guy seemed to like that. It reminded me of Bridget Jones, which I'd seen at the cinema a few weeks previously, when Mark Darcy tells Bridget "I like you very much, just as you are". I was being my very un-French, loud, talkative, sweary, burping and farting, telling it like it is Brit girl, and he liked it. More than that he'd dumped someone else to be with that. I didn't think I could be happier.

The next morning as I drove to work I plugged in my earpiece and called Nikki from the traffic jam I was stuck in. As she picked up I sang to her "I've met my future husband!!!" to which she replied "Fuck off! You haven't even slept with him yet!". Nikki was convinced it was just a rebound but I *knew* this was something else, something different. And it didn't matter if she believed me or not.

Over the next few months Ben and I fell in love with each other in a big way, culminating in us deciding to move in together just 3 months after we met, and escalating to us shocking the hell out of our friends shortly after.

On 22nd June 2002 we were on holiday in Corsica and it was boiling hot. We couldn't do anything or go anywhere as the whole area was experiencing a crazy heat wave of 35°C+, so we spent most days in the apartment complex's swimming pool, just chatting (and snogging!). On that particular day we were talking about weddings, and had been for a few days, as we were invited to Ben's family friend's wedding the following month. There was lots of "when I get married I want xyz" which ended in us both looking at each other, as we stood in this swimming pool, and saying "shall we do it?!".

And that was all either of us needed as a proposal. Just 6 months and 21 days after we met in a bar in Nice we decided to spend the rest of our life together. And neither of us had a shadow of a doubt that it was the right decision.

As we announced it to friends and family on returning home we got a very mixed review. Pretty much all of our friends thought we were crazy; my friends thought it was a severe case of rebound, and his friends couldn't begin to understand why a 26 year old guy would want to tie himself down. However our parents were on our side from the start. My mum told me she could see how right he was for me, and she didn't care how long we'd known each other as her and my dad got engaged after a similar length of time (although it was far less shocking back then of course); Ben's mum told us that she could see that "*on avait trouvé chaussure à notre pied*" as the French say ("we had found the shoe that fits our foot").

What I especially loved was that, even though Ben wasn't overly comfortable in English at that stage, he arranged to call my parents, to have them both on the phone at the same time, to ask for my hand in marriage (even if it was a bit late as we'd got engaged in a swimming pool in Corsica!). As my dad said in his father of the bride speech at our wedding "it was an offer I couldn't refuse!".

We got married 1 year, 8 months and 2 days after we met. Lots of our friends thought it wouldn't last, that we were rushing into it, that we didn't know each other enough, that we didn't know what we were doing. But as I write this we are just over one month off from celebrating our 16th wedding anniversary, so we're not doing too badly… and I'm pleased to say that despite people not being sure it would last they threw themselves into the wedding and we had our perfect day.

Task - how to be open to miracles

I used to think that miracles were mythical and didn't happen to actual people. Then one random, nondescript, Saturday night I went out for drinks and met the man who would change my whole life around. I know it sounds corny to talk about soulmates, but that's exactly what he was / is. Something clicked and it was as if our paths and our lives up to that point had been leading us towards each other.

Ever since then I've been open to anything being possible in life. In my personal and professional life. This means I go for things, talk to people, put myself out there, as I know that anything is possible BUT you've got to be in it to win it as the saying goes.

Do you believe that miracles can happen and that anything is possible in life? Or are you quite closed to these ideas? Do you automatically assume that you won't win that thing / get that promotion / meet that perfect guy?

If you want miracles to show up in your life you have to be open to them. You have to believe it's possible for you. And I mean REALLY believe, don't just pay lip service and be all "yeah, yeah, I believe", you've got to believe right down into your gut. Because when you believe, your eyes are open in a completely different way.

About 6 years ago I read "The Luck Factor" by Richard Wiseman which proves this to be true. One of my big takeaways from this book is that if you see yourself as a lucky person then you SEE things that 'unlucky' people don't, you DO things that 'unlucky' people don't. Maybe you see money on the floor that 'unlucky' people don't, maybe you strike up a conversation with a stranger that leads to a new job, a business contract, a relationship.

So you have to BELIEVE that miracles can and do happen, so that you are aware and open to them, and so they can show up in your life.

This means being aware in your life - aware of your surroundings, the people around you, the signs on the wall, the adverts on the bus stop - seeing and observing EVERYTHING that goes on around you. That's how I started chatting to a random man in a bar one night who went on to become my husband. That's how I ended up as a Psychologies Magazine ambassador, because I was open enough to see information about it, and then to apply and be accepted. And a million and one other miraculous situations in my life.

Are you ready to accept miracles into your life?

To be open to miracles in your life you need to remain upbeat, positive and open-minded. To help you feel like this every day make sure you grab my free book bonuses, in particular the checklist of how to be happy, and the motivational audio. Get your bonuses here: www.SophieLeBrozec.com/happy-bonus

The one where I miscarried in the middle of nowhere

It was lunchtime on the 14th July 2005, France's national holiday, and I was just over the border in Switzerland, having an absolutely wonderful time. Ben and I were on holiday with my parents, his mum and his gran, at a place he'd been going to ever since he was 3 years old. Everything was perfect and I was so happy. But as our lunch at a lakeside restaurant went on I started to worry. I was beginning to feel that tell-tale cramp that every woman knows means her period is coming. Except just a week previously I had had a positive pregnancy test. So there shouldn't be any period coming. Well not for 9 months anyway. I didn't dare go to the toilet, I was worried about what I might find. But eventually I forced myself to get up, to put one foot in front of the other, to see what I feared might be revealed.

As I pulled my jeans and knickers down a silent sob caught in my throat. There was blood there. And not just the spotting that I'd read about in my pregnancy and fertility books. This did not bode well. But we were in Switzerland (where I had no health insurance), just across the border in France everyone was on holiday, so I put a smile on my face (and toilet roll in my knickers), washed my hands and went back to my family of holiday-makers.

The plan for the afternoon was to walk around the beautiful *Chateau de Chillon*, but I wasn't there, I was in my head, asking myself a million different questions - was this a miscarriage? Maybe it was twins and I was miscarrying one (which is what my mum is pretty certain happened to her when she was pregnant with me)? Maybe this was all normal and I was worrying about nothing?

The questions spun around in my head, tumbling over each other, fighting for answers that I didn't have. Eventually I pulled my mum to one side and told her what was happening, as a nurse, trained midwife and mum of 5, I knew she would know what to do. But sadly there was nothing we could do until I could have a scan and either confirm or deny what we feared.

I had to wait until the next day to be scanned, and that evening I ping-ponged between the depths of sadness and irrational hope. The fact that the cramps and bleeding were increasing didn't help.

The next morning I lay on my back as a random gynaecologist in the nearest town inserted the sonographic wand inside me and I wanted to curl up in a corner and cry. Because I knew it before he even pronounced the words. My baby was gone. It was clinical, it was medical. There were no words of comfort. I was a statistic. It wasn't a big deal. I was young. I could try again. And, he told me, luckily it was leaving my body naturally. But I didn't feel lucky at the time.

I knew NO ONE who had had a miscarriage and I felt such shame. Such guilt. I had one job, to keep our baby safe for 9 months, and I hadn't even been able to do it for 2 weeks. What kind of mum would I be?!? I heard the statistics that 1 in 4 pregnancies ends in miscarriage, but how was that possible when I didn't know a soul who had miscarried? No, I was alone in this. No one knew how I felt. No one had ever been such a bad pregnant woman and miscarried.

Ben drove us round the winding bends of the French Alps on our way back to our mountain chalet and I cried silent tears. I had been the most excited of my life that brief time I'd been pregnant. And now I felt empty, hollow, filled with grey clouds of sadness. I heard the "well at least you got pregnant" and the "you can try again" and the "these things happen" but they all made me feel worse. I wanted THIS baby. WHY? What had I done? It wasn't fair.

We hadn't wanted to try for a baby straight away after getting married, we were too young and still had lots we wanted to do. Once all our ducks were in a row, and we were ready to move into a new house we decided to start trying. Amazingly (after 13 years on the pill) I got pregnant the first month. I found out the day before we went on holiday; we hadn't wanted to hide it from people but wanted to tell family first. I only told my boss as I knew he'd be so happy for us (he was) and then we told our parents and siblings. We planned to tell our friends when we got back from our holiday. Except there was nothing to tell by then.

I didn't feel ready to share with them that I was a big, fat failure who couldn't carry out the most simplest of nature's tasks. I spent the rest of that summer licking my wounds, feeling such grief for what should have been and never would be. The only way I could console myself was by telling myself that I would get pregnant the next month we tried, I mean how easy had it been?!? Ignorance is bliss they say…

Maybe that first time was a fluke, maybe a hormone surge coming off the pill, maybe, who fricking knows? But month after month just when I started thinking about doing pregnancy tests I would feel those all too familiar cramps and know that this time was not our time.

And month after month friends announced their pregnancies. Everyone around me was pregnant and it just wasn't fair. For half of them it was by bloody accident! They didn't deserve it - we were trying, we were ready, they weren't! I started to feel bitter towards everyone.

As if that weren't enough well-meaning older colleagues would ask me when we were going to have a baby, and remind me "don't keep hanging around, you're nearly 30, tick-tock, tick-tock" and to ask me "what are you waiting for?". Some days I would float up out of my body, look down on our conversation and imagine how they would react if I screamed at them "I'm bloody trying, but I've had a miscarriage and it's not working!". Instead I nodded my head, smiled and said "yes, soon, probably" and hoped I was right.

From my miscarriage to my positive pregnancy test with Léna took 8 months, and whilst I hear that this is quite normal and average, it felt like the longest 8 months of my life. With the next 9 months being a rollercoaster of excitement and fear. Every week I remained pregnant was a week closer to viability, every kick was a reassurance there was a live baby in there. But every time my pregnancy symptoms faded or things went quiet in my belly my fear came rushing back in.

Task - how to deal with shame

When I miscarried I felt a constant all-encompassing feeling of shame. Such shame that I wasn't able to do this one simple, basic thing. Ben was sad but didn't understand why I felt this way. He's a mathematician so for him it was a case of statistics, if 1 in 4 (or 1 in 3 or 1 in 5 depending on what stats you look at) pregnancies ends in miscarriage then the odds are quite high that you will have a miscarriage. It's not some rare, unexpected disease. As far as he was concerned this one wasn't meant to be, nature was dealing with a baby that wouldn't have made it anyway, and we could / should just move on to the next pregnancy.

For me it was so personal. I couldn't believe those stats as I knew no one who had miscarried, which made me into a big, fat failure. I carried that shame round with me every day, wondering how people would judge me if they knew. The thing is, because we hadn't told any of our friends that I was pregnant, no one knew I had miscarried, so I didn't feel like I could suddenly share about my miscarriage. Instead I carried the pain of shame around with me until I finally got pregnant with Léna. I breathed a sigh of relief and immediately proceeded to tell the world about our wonderful news, but also about my miscarriage story. The pee wasn't even dry on my pregnancy test when I announced to the world and his wife that we were having a baby. I explained that I was telling everyone early as I couldn't bear to miscarry 'alone' again.

And my shame disappeared. Just like that. By sharing my story it was gone. Over.

Similarly when I found out Cédric was cheating on me with his colleague I felt such shame. I couldn't bear to tell anyone, instead I let the shame eat me up from the inside out. It nearly drove me to take my own life, I was so mortified and felt such shame. It stayed inside me until I bit the bullet and sent a mass email to all my family and friends telling them we were over, and the basics of what had happened. As I hit 'send' the shame left me.

Now I'm not telling you to take your shame and mass-mail the planet about it. But I do massively recommend sharing your shame. When you keep it inside of you it grows and thrives. It makes you feel worse and worse. It morphs into a giant monster that you have no control over. It ruins your health and can end up ruining your life.

So take your shame - and your courage - into your hands, and share. Start with a person you have absolute faith and trust in. Your mum / a mother figure. Your best friend. Your sister. Your partner. It doesn't matter who, as long as it's someone who has your best interest at heart. Tell them what happened and why you feel this shame. If need be you can tell your story to others. Or maybe just sharing it once is all you need to get rid of this weighty emotion. It doesn't matter. All that matters is that you get that evil monster out of you, as quickly as possible.

Most of the women in my Life Reboot Camp community arrive carrying shame in a suitcase (or removal van for some of them). Little by little they know they are in a safe place and can share with this group of strangers. These women who only want the best for themselves and for others. These women who have each other's back with a strength I have never seen before. Life Reboot Campers have confessed to being tangled up in abusive relationships, to feeling like a failure at work, to no longer feeling attracted to their husbands, to not enjoying spending time with their kids and so much more.

We need a safe space to be able to share and get rid of our shame. To know we are not alone. To know that we are loved and supported. Make sure you find someone or somewhere where you can feel safe, where you can share your shame and set that burden down.
And know that both I and the Life Reboot Camp community are there if that feels like the right place for you.

The one where I nearly died after childbirth

"This wasn't what I had planned" I raged in my head as yet another contraction wreaked havoc throughout my imprisoned body, I tried moving away from the pain but it was coming from inside of me, and I was strapped to the bed by numerous threads. There was a drip in my arm, a baby heart rate monitor strapped to my belly and a contraction detector (that might not be the official term) hooked up to another part of my tummy.

Labouring to bring Léna into the world was pretty much the exact opposite of my birth plan. Which just goes to show that the best laid plans often do go awry. MY plan had been to have my mum in the labour room with me. At the time Ben and I were living in the south of France and my parents were in the UK; we agreed that my mum would come out for two weeks and hopefully we would time this around Baby Number 1 deciding to make an appearance. Unfortunately Léna didn't get that memo.

My mum came out a couple of days before I was 40 weeks pregnant and we thought we'd be pretty safe. I was convinced if the baby showed no sign of wanting to join us that I could easily smoke her out with brisk walks, bumpy car rides, raspberry leaf tea tablets and eating hot curries. In a personality that I have come to know and love over the last 12 and a bit years, Léna put her foot down and said "NO! I'm not coming out yet!"

Despite attempting everything to get birth going there was still no sign of our baby. For some reason in France your due date is pretty much 42 weeks of pregnancy, and if you get that far then they induce you immediately. So different to the UK where I was offered sweeps from 40 weeks to encourage things to start happening.

For the two weeks that my mum was with us I did have a lovely time though. It was wonderful to chat to her about parenting, what to do, her parenting experiences and just generally everything and anything for 2 whole weeks. I vividly remember asking her "but how do you know what's the right thing to do when there are so many different schools of thought on the 'right' way to parent a baby? Should you let them cry it out or go to them? How do you know what is right?!?" I remember what she said to me so clearly. It's just a shame I didn't have enough faith to put it into practice when the time came...

Mum told me "no one knows your baby better than you, and one thing I've learnt from having 5 babies is that I know nothing about babies because they're all so different. You have to trust that you'll know what the right thing is for your baby, listen to your instincts."

She then went on to tell me that I had one sister who as a baby had to be soothed immediately; if you didn't, her crying would crescendo into hysteria. However the other sister, born just over a year later would cry for a short while and then go back to sleep by herself if left. And that no book can teach you what a mother instinctively knows about her own baby.

At the time I was reassured as I was pretty good with my instinct, the problem came once Léna arrived, the safe comfort of my mum was a whole country away and I was trying to figure my baby out seemingly on my own.

It was with tears in my eyes that I accompanied Mum to the airport 2 weeks after her arrival with my baby still tucked up safe and sound in the warmth of my belly. I couldn't believe she was going home, empty-handed as it were. I felt like I'd failed in some unspoken test already as, according to UK dates I was "late".

Two days later it was my French due date which signalled an appointment with my gynaecologist who was also my obstetrician for this pregnancy (yes in France you have an actual doctor who follows you right through your pregnancy, childbirth and post-natal check-ups!). She scanned me and told me the baby was small and that my placenta was deteriorating so she wanted to induce me the next day and booked us in for 9am.

When we got home I got out my birth plan and crossed out the first thing on the list: "I don't want to be induced". The next things were:

- I don't want a drip
- I don't want an epidural
- I don't want an episiotomy
- I don't want a C-section.

There were lots of "don't wants" as French childbirth is quite different to the UK, in that you have very little say in what happens, and it tends to be very medicalised. In general you lie on a bed, feet in stirrups and attempt to defy nature and gravity as you push!

Ben took a photo of me as we were getting ready for bed, my last pregnant photo. Whilst I was gutted that I was going to be induced I was so excited to know that the next day I was going to meet my baby finally. I was blissfully ignorant of the fact that inductions can take more than a day, and incredibly lucky that mine didn't. I was also blissfully ignorant of other serious labour complications which I was to come across in just 24 hours time.

We got to the hospital on time and I felt like a fraud walking in unaided and not bent over with contractions. I had visions of how my labour would be having seen hundreds of births on TV and in films, yet here I was walking in with no sign of labour at all.

They got us ready for the delivery room; I was given a rather delightful hospital gown to labour in and Ben had to wear an ER-style gown and face mask as he had a slight cold. They told us we couldn't take anything in to the room with us as it was a sterile environment, so no books, music, nothing to take my mind off the contractions or what I was about to go through. However as we were about to leave the locker room with all our belongings behind us, they reminded us "don't forget your camera so you can take photos once your baby is born", it wasn't until afterwards that either of us realised how ridiculous that was having been refused an iPod and books for lack of sterility!

Luckily I didn't have a clue what to expect from an induction (in France or in the UK) because otherwise I might not have shown up. They got me to lie on my back on a bed with stirrups, ready to give birth when the time came. They strapped one sensor to my tummy where Léna was, to monitor her heart rate, and another sensor to keep track of my contractions. Next up was the drip so they could start to pump me with oxytocin to trick my body into thinking it was in labour. What nobody warned me is that doing this is not like a gentle build-up to labour; you go from "everything's fine, I'm chatting and laughing with everyone around me" to "kapow! What the fuck was that pain?!?" Because your body isn't actually ready to labour yet.

So basically now I had to lie on my back, strapped to this bed, with NOTHING to take my mind off the contractions (they're not so into antenatal classes either in France so I hadn't been taught anything about breathing, visualising, relaxing or anything like that). No TV, no music, no books, just me, Ben, a midwife or two and a very sterile hospital room.

I told Ben he had to entertain me, to which he started trying to do George Clooney impressions due to his ER outfit. Let's just say his impressions were not cutting it on that day.

Despite having had to cross "no induction" and "no drip" off my birth plan I was still determined not to have to give into an epidural. I knew in France there was a lot of pressure to have epidurals and I really didn't want one.

Within 10 minutes of the first contraction I was already offered an epidural, which I politely refused. 20 minutes later they offered it to me again after examining me and telling me I was 3cm dilated. This time I explained that there was no need to offer it to me as I wanted a natural birth, and I was going to try without an epidural. I got raised eyebrows in response but they didn't try and argue with me.

After 2 ½ hours of labouring, of full-on contractions every 1-2 minutes, which I had to take on the chin lying down, with no music, no books, no moving around etc they examined me and informed me that I hadn't made any progress in the last hour despite all the contractions. Through gritted teeth (yes I know NOW this is not the best way to deal with pain!) I reminded them "no epidurals thanks!", to which they said to Ben "your wife has got very strong willpower".

For some reason they don't offer you anything else in France - no paracetamol, no gas and air, nothing, in fact I wasn't even allowed to eat or drink anything in case I needed a general anaesthetic to deliver the baby, not even any water.

Finally 3 hours after everything started my obstetrician came to see me and informed me that I seemed to be blocked at 3cm because my waters hadn't broken. No shit Sherlock! I was lying on my back with synthetic oxytocin being pumped around my body. The baby wasn't pushing on them and I wasn't active to get things moving. I asked if I could get up to get some action going and everyone looked at me in shock, at which stage I realised I was going to be strapped down until this baby came out, however long it took.

I asked my doctor what my options were. I had two it turned out. Either I could keep up this obstinance of no epidural; the contractions would keep coming thick and fast but I was unlikely to dilate any further, the baby would end up getting distressed and it would mean an emergency C-section. Or I could have an epidural, they would break my waters, this would move labour along and the baby would be born 'naturally'.

It turns out in France they won't break your waters unless you have had an epidural, it is thought to be too painful otherwise. I tried explaining that it was fine, as it couldn't be much worse than the pain I was currently going through, but still they refused. It was only afterwards talking to my mum (a trained midwife) that I found out this is absolute rubbish.

I asked them to give me some time to think, and I tried to come to terms with my whole birth being so far from my dream and my birth plan. Whilst dealing with this in my head I had an almighty contraction during which I might or might not have bitten Ben's hand. At which time he might or might not have said to the midwife in the room "epidural over here please!".

I finally realised it was time to give in. I was already so tired and at just 3cm dilated I knew I was a long way from the finish line. I finally snapped "get me the bloody epidural then!" or possibly even ruder words.

It was a very strange feeling when the epidural coursed through my body because I didn't feel any different. What did happen is that I stopped feeling the contractions, first of all I panicked that they had stopped altogether and there was a problem with the baby, then I watched the monitor I was hooked up to, spiking with another contraction, and I realised I couldn't feel them anymore. At all.

They broke my waters and I started to feel sleepy, it had been an emotional morning fighting the medical staff and dealing with the non-stop contractions. It was 12.30pm so I suggested Ben go and grab a bite to eat, call our parents with an update and I'd have a nap.

I woke up well over an hour later and announced to the room in general "I really need to poo!" the midwife who'd been keeping an eye on me did a quick examination and told me I was fully dilated, and that she would find my husband and the doctor. As she left the room I sat there incredulously and counted on my hands; 3 hours of on-going contractions which resulted in just 3cm dilation, then an epidural, water breaking, an hour-long nap and I was ready to give birth. It was mad.

Ben arrived with a couple of midwives who told me I needed to wait some more as the doctor was on her way, I informed them in no uncertain terms that this baby was coming and I was done waiting. I started pushing and (so I was told later) 12 minutes later Léna was born, apparently the midwives have a 'race' to see whose mum is fastest and I won that day!

Just as Léna's head was crowning my doctor arrived wielding some kind of surgical scissors, announcing "time for the episiotomy!". Before I had time to object a midwife interjected "it's too late, she's already torn". It felt like a small victory for Léna and me.

My doctor did get to deliver our first baby though and as she placed a tiny, healthy 5lb 15oz baby into my arms and told me "*c'est une fille*" (it's a girl), I burst into tears. I'd done it. It had been so hard, but I'd done it. One thing I'd been adamant about was that I wanted to do skin-to-skin and to breastfeed immediately unless they could give me a very good reason that our baby's health was at risk and they needed to whisk her away.

I felt like I knew Léna as soon as she was put on my chest, and she seemed to know exactly what she was doing as I put her to my breast, she started sucking and seemed at ease.

It was time for photos, for tears, for kisses, for laughing and joking. For not actually caring how she got here, just that she was finally here, and perfectly healthy. After a while one of the midwives suggested we put a nappy on her, as she was still naked against my bare skin, under a blanket. As we lifted the blanket we realised it was too late, the two of us were covered in meconium (a sticky, tar-like poo that newborns do shortly after birth). Whoops!

Léna was born at 2.12pm on a Friday which was great as it meant our working parents could come and visit her the next day as it was the weekend. By around 5pm we were in my hospital room, which I was sharing with another mum and her baby daughter who'd been born just a few hours before Léna. Our room was essentially a hotel room, with en-suite bathroom and changing tables, it certainly felt very luxurious after everything I'd experienced with the NHS (National Health Service) in the UK.

I was feeling good as I pottered around the room, getting settled in, like I do when on holiday. I got my toiletries bag out, found my brand-new hospital pyjamas and slippers, and got snuggly. Léna was having cuddles with Ben and his twin brother, Nico, who had come by after work. I was going to be staying in for 5 days so I wanted to feel "at home".

Around 8pm or 9pm it was time for the visitors to leave. Suddenly I found myself alone with the baby I had known so well on the inside, who was now on the outside, plus a relatively strange woman (we had met at the hospital's attempts at antenatal classes - basically having us float in a 38°C pool) and her newborn baby.

The next few hours were spent breastfeeding, changing nappies, replying to text messages, chatting to my roommate and staring at my beautiful baby. Léna was in her crib as I was doing some last pottering and tidying away of things before calling it a day (it was nearly midnight after all) when suddenly I felt this gush. Down below.

My instant thought was that I'd wet myself. My sister had warned me that after having a baby you had little control over your bruised and battered lady parts and that this wasn't uncommon, so I was embarrassed but not too worried as I looked down. Until I saw what looked like a scene from a chainsaw massacre - my lovely new pjs and slippers were COVERED in blood.

I casually went over to the en suite bathroom, for some reason I was ashamed, like I'd done something wrong. I pulled my knickers down, and saw that the brick-like post-labour sanitary towel was sodden with blood. As I sat on the toilet it sounded like I was peeing but the noise was blood flowing into the bowl. I didn't know what to do, I knew heavy bleeding was common after giving birth, but blood flowing out of you like urine didn't seem right.

I grabbed the emergency phone that was to the right of me as I sat bleeding into the toilet and spoke to the midwife on duty. I told her that I thought something was wrong as I was bleeding A LOT and could she come and check me out. I got a very condescending "*Madame*, it is normal to bleed lots after having a baby.".

That was me told. Then I heard Léna start to cry and I gave myself a pep talk, it went something like this "pull yourself together! You're a mum now and your baby has to come first." I grabbed a fresh sanitary towel, fully aware that it would be drenched in seconds, pulled my knickers and pyjama bottoms up over my blood-soaked legs, washed my hands whilst leaning on the sink, surveying my ghostly white face, and slowly walked the ten steps back to my bed and baby Léna.

At the halfway point I nearly passed out and had to more or less throw myself at the bed as I needed something to hold onto. My roommate asked if I was ok and I quickly told her what had happened; as I simultaneously cuddled Léna to me to soothe her tears I picked up the phone by my bed to ring the midwife again.

I started to explain the problem, again, and I was cut off with "*Madame*, I've already told you heavy bleeding is normal" in a very patronising and 'these new mothers!' voice. And I lost my shit.

"I nearly just passed out and I have never even come close to that in my entire life, I am bleeding like its pee and you WILL COME AND EXAMINE ME NOW!"

The midwife huffed and puffed and said she would come but it was a waste of time, blah, blah. She certainly didn't rush and made it very clear that I was a neurotic new mum who needed to get her shit together. She did the standard bleeding check of pushing down on my uterus and blood gushed out, at the same time her face paled.

"You're haemorrhaging and we need to get you into the operating room now!" she told me, suddenly all business. She wanted to know when I'd last eaten (they couldn't do a general anaesthetic as I'd had a yogurt a few hours before) and if I was breastfeeding (so I could put Léna to my breast as this helps the uterus to contract).

She rushed off to call my doctor and came back with a drip in her hands. She was so flustered she broke the drip needle in my wrist as she attempted to put it in, and then it took her three more goes to get it right. When it was done she unceremoniously wrenched Léna from my breast, putting her back in her crib and telling me that the women from the nursery would come and take her there while I was being operated on. I remember yelling to my roommate as I was whisked out of the room "don't let them give her a bottle!".

I remember being run down the hospital corridors as the midwife asked me if I wanted to call my husband. I'd been thinking about this ever since she'd mentioned operating theatre, but we lived a 45 minute drive from the hospital, it was gone midnight and he was likely already asleep. It was also chucking it down with rain and nearly all the roads were winding, unlit country roads. So I told her no, I didn't want to call my husband and have him die in a car crash rushing to get to me. I asked her if there was any reason to call him, to which she shrugged and said "to tell him goodbye, just in case".

I mean what the actual fuck?!? I was 30 years old. I had just given birth to my first baby and had no loved ones in the hospital with me. Blood was gushing out of me, making me faint, I was being rushed into theatre but only because I insisted that something was wrong, and then I hear that I might die! Yay, talk about great bedside manner.

I told her that no, I still didn't want to call him, but that they could bring me a phone afterwards and I would call him then.

The operating theatre was like a fridge and I started shaking as soon as I was wheeled in, I was just dressed in a backless gown which did nothing to protect me from the cold, plus the blood loss and shock were kicking in. I was full-on head to toe shaking as my doctor from that afternoon explained they were going to give me a spinal block, to numb all feelings from the waist down, so she could examine me and see if any placenta was left inside or if there was a clot or something.

The anaesthesiologist berated me for shaking and barked at me to stop so he could put the needle in, "or do you want to end up paralysed?!?" he admonished. This had been my big fear with the epidural, yes I wanted a natural birth, but equally I was afraid of a needle going into my spine and something going wrong. And here I was with that exact fear being spelled out to me. The actual medical person responsible for sticking a needle in my spine had just described what I had been so worried about.

With every ounce of strength and willpower I forced myself not to move. Easier said than done as my mind was like a horror movie as it flashed through the initial gush of blood loss, the sound of blood free-flowing into the toilet, seeing my baby howl as she was pulled from my breast and I was whisked away. And the soundtrack on repeat in my head was "do you want to call your husband? To say goodbye!" and "do you want to end up paralysed?".

Finally I lost all feeling in my legs and upwards to my waist, but joy, I could still move the upper part of my body, I wasn't paralysed. My legs were akimbo and my doctor was wrist deep inside me as she rooted around to see what was going on. Fortunately I'm not a prude and am comfortable in my skin and in my body, because I seemed to be in some kind of Grand Central Station for medical personnel at the hospital that night. I lay with my legs wide apart opposite the door, so that the numerous people who casually wandered in and out got a full pornographic view of what I normally try to keep private.

At one point I was very close to asking if there was anyone in this town who **hadn't** seen my *foufoune* that night!

Eventually the doctor told me she couldn't find anything and it was just one of those things, maybe it had been a clot that had burst, and that I was borderline for needing a blood transfusion but that I should be ok. Again I wanted to shout out "just as well I bloody insisted there was something wrong then, isn't it?!?"

They wheeled me to a nearby labour room to be monitored before I could go back up to my room and be reunited with Léna. And I finally got to place my call to Ben, waking him up at 3am but I needed to talk to him. As I explained what had happened through sobs I kept repeating over and over "it's all ok now, DON'T COME!". I was terrified he would get in the car and try and come and see me in the heavy rain, killing himself in the process.

I hung up and cried and cried as the full weight and emotions of the past 24 hours washed over me. Then I started to hear noises, I was in a labour room and I could hear a woman going through her own personal bittersweet torture as she brought her baby into the world. And I cried some more. Why did something so wonderful have to come about in such a brutal way? I had so much sympathy for women over the centuries who had brought their babies into the world in such scary circumstances. I had been very lucky.

It was only when I was back home a week or so later, that I read the number 1 cause of a mother dying in childbirth is haemorrhaging. Something I was grateful to have been blissfully ignorant of.

The one where I sunk into postnatal depression

My radio alarm clock showed 3.04am, our bedroom was pitch black apart from the glow from the clock and the muted street light through the slats of our shutter. The only sound was that of Ben's slow, sleep-filled breathing beside me. Silent tear after silent tear slipped from the corner of my eye down the side of my face and into my ear, but I couldn't be bothered to wipe them away or to move even. It wasn't the first night I'd spent this way and I knew it wouldn't be the last either. I didn't dare wake Ben up or tell him during the day; we were both busy trying to get our business off the ground and I didn't want to worry him as he had enough on his plate already.

I thought back to how many waking hours I'd had with 4 month old Léna the day before. We'd had less than an hour together in the morning before she'd gone to the childminder's, then just over 1 hour together in the evening before she fell asleep.

My mind returned to its constant worry - how much milk I had expressed that day. I hadn't realised that you don't produce as much milk when you pump as when you nurse a baby directly, and the amount I was pumping got less and less every day. But I was convinced I had to exclusively breastfeed her until she was 6 months old, and then she could try solid foods and maybe take one formula feed a day at that stage. Day after day I sat at my desk, silently weeping for my absent daughter, as my Avent electric breast pump made its electronic noises and my daughter's lifeline flowed from my breast into a plastic bottle. It all felt so wrong. So unnatural. The complete opposite of what I thought motherhood would be like, and I was so sad.

There were no new mothers' groups around as most mums in France go back to work when their children are 2-4 months old, so I was very average and normal when 3 month old Léna started at the childminder's. All my friends lived at least 45 minutes away and only 1 or 2 of them were mums, everyone else felt like they were on a different planet, with different lives, needs, habits and routines.

My mum was miles away, across a whole country and a sea in the UK and I felt so alone.

I told no one. Because I couldn't put it into words. I also didn't know if this was normal or not, and I don't think I wanted to know either. I just wanted to keep putting one foot in front of the other until I came out the other side of this, which I just assumed I would, one day or another.

My weight dropped severely as I was either breastfeeding or expressing my milk 24/7, and so anything that came into my body went straight out in the form of breast milk. I hadn't really noticed it until a friend pulled me aside and asked if I was ok, as she'd only ever seen me that skinny once before - when Cédric ended it with me. I told her I was fine but it was the wake-up call I needed, and things started to turn around after that day.

It was only 6 years later, as I laughed and snuggled my 6 month old baby, so full of complete joy, that I suddenly realised THIS was normal. This was right. What I had gone through with Léna wasn't right, and I should have said something, done something, seen someone. It took me 6 years to realise it, and I felt so sad for myself as I realised how much easier and better things could have been if I'd had the necessary support. I hugged both my girls just a little bit tighter that night and told my younger self I was sorry.

Task - how to ask for help

If I had been able to ask for help, if I'd known how to, I am certain I wouldn't have suffered this way after Léna was born. But I was embarrassed. I felt like every mum I knew or passed on the street had her shit together. It was 2007 and social media was barely a thing, it certainly was not a place for mums to share how crappy they were feeling or how badly they thought they were parenting. I felt like I should just keep going, head down into the oncoming wind of parenting, hormones and the not knowing of child-rearing. I didn't know that if I asked for help things would get better, not worse. There was an irrational part of me that told me my baby would be taken away from me if I shared what was going on. So I stayed quiet. I kept up the façade. Until I got called out on it. And then I finally breathed a sigh of relief.

Someone had noticed, but I sometimes wonder what might have happened if no one had picked up on the fact things weren't going well. And that's when I realised I needed to be able to ask for help next time round.

I have the most incredible support network - a husband, parents, siblings, friends and more, but for some reason I don't like to tell them when I need help. When things aren't going well these are rarely the people I turn to. So I will be forever grateful for the people who created social media, because for all that I hate it, this is where I go when I need help. When I was pregnant with Clémence and after her birth my helpline of choice was Twitter, with its assortment of online mum friends who were there 24/7 thanks to where they were in the world and their sleepless babies.

Now I have graduated to Facebook groups. I am in a few paid ones with the most incredibly supportive women. That's where I go to get my help these days. Whether it's a confidence crisis, struggling with feeling low, questions, issues, problems or worries. I turn to the comfort of 'strangers'. When I say 'strangers' I mean women I've never met in real life, but who know me better than most people who've known me my entire life.

It is imperative that you understand the importance of asking for help. You are not alone. Everyone is going through their own kind of shit, some are just better at hiding it than others. So ask. Who can you turn to? Your partner? Mum? Best friend? Boss? Neighbour? Colleague? Sister? Or an online group? Community?

If you need help and have no one you can turn to please email me at support@sophielebrozec.com, tell me what country you live in, what is going on with you and I will do my best to find you help where you live.

And don't forget that in the Life Reboot Camp community you get this support and more, if that feels like something you need or want.

The one with my first failed business

It was in January 2004 during our honeymoon to the Maldives that I first noticed the change in Ben. Instead of reading his usual murder mystery books by the pool he was poring over Richard Branson's 'Losing my virginity'. Then he started talking about wanting to set up his own business. I ignored this subject of conversation for as long as I possibly could. Until finally I realised this policy wasn't making it go away, so I asked him what was going on.

"I want to set up my own business, be my own boss" he replied to me with a grin on his face.

Oh fuck! What did this mean for me? We had a really nice life, we earned more than we needed from good, steady jobs that didn't require us to renounce our life in exchange for a salary. I thought we were both in the same place of wanting to live life, do the work we had to in order to get paid every month, but that was that.

It turned out that Ben had other ideas. He didn't just want to crawl up an employee career ladder, very slowly, he wanted to be in control of his life, which meant setting up and running his own business.

This scared the crap out of me. As far as I was concerned people who ran their own businesses were mad, there was zero security and it was the opposite of what I wanted for me, my marriage, my future family. How had this crept up on me?

I tried to talk Ben round, bigging up the several weeks of paid holiday that we both had, job security for life (pretty much), zero stress. But he was determined.

For nearly 2 years it was a bone of contention between the two of us. He wanted to set up his own business, I didn't want him to. I honestly could not understand WHY he wanted to do this.

That all changed in October 2005 in Sri Lanka. We were on holiday there, with Ben's mum and brother, Nico. On the second day I cried off from the organised outing as I wanted to laze and read by the pool. As I waved goodbye to Ben the title of one of his holiday books caught my eye "Rich Dad Poor Dad: What the Rich Teach Their Kids About Money That the Poor and Middle Class Do Not!", curiosity piqued, I took it to the pool with me. And I absorbed it. I could not put the thing down.

Ben came back to our hotel room at the end of the day to my - rather startling - announcement "I want to set up my own business too!". Talk about doing a 360!

The book had made me look at things differently, at a time when I was all over the shop trying (and failing) to get pregnant, this made me realise that I could take control of my life, and that if I wanted kids then it would be good to have flexibility around them and around my work.

Of course the next question was WHAT business??? And this was the biggie, neither of us had a clue. We also had no business network and no one to turn to and ask, everyone we knew had "safe" stable jobs.

Over the next few months we got chatting to the one person we knew who ran his own business and he shared a great idea that he was certain would work for us. A luxury travel agency, organising bespoke holidays on the French Riviera where we lived. With Ben's knowledge of IT and travel, and my expertise in customer service, marketing and PR it was the perfect combination.

Little by little as I grew a baby in my tummy Ben and I grew the idea of a luxury travel agency; and around the same time Léna was born we both chucked in our jobs and launched LE BROZEC.

However before we even got to that stage we went through nearly a whole year of hair-pulling anxiety about whether to go for it or not. Both sets of parents are risk-averse, we knew nothing about business and knew no one in business. We had no network and no contacts, as suppliers or clients. What we did have however was the will to make it work and the ignorance of youth.

We drew up lists of pros and cons. We debated the worst case scenario and looked at what we had to lose. We spent late nights talking about resentment over doing a job you hate and deathbed regrets.

It came down to this - we could go for it, we could leave our safe, well-paid, guaranteed-for-life jobs and set up our own business. It would mean re-negotiating our mortgage for a short period, it would mean needing a back-up plan, it would mean learning to live on as little money as possible (at the same time as welcoming our first baby into the world - something that is commonly known to come at a certain cost!). But it was doable.

Before we could make a final decision we had to have our back-up plan in place, which is what brought me to a crazy phone conversation with my parents one evening, aged 30 years old and 6 months pregnant with my first baby.

Me: "Hi Mum! Can I ask a favour? Ben and I want to set up our own business but we need to have a back-up plan if it all fails. Which it totally won't as it's going to be amazing. Yeah, so if it all goes horribly wrong - which it won't - please can me, Ben, the baby, the dog and the cat all come and move in with you in England?"

My mum: "What? Er, well you know, we'll always be here for you if you need us. The dog and the cat too? Um, yeah, ok, we'll figure it out."

Me to Ben: "Yay! We have our back-up plan in place - not that we're ever going to need it. This is going to be HUGE!"

Famous last words from the ignorance of youth…

We threw ourselves into setting up our new business and it was so exciting working together on something we were both so passionate about. Although working with a newborn baby was far from a walk in the park. I was completely torn between wanting to spend time with her, soak her up and just spend hours snuggling with her, and wanting our business to get off the ground.

I allowed myself the first month to recover, get settled with Léna at home, with breastfeeding and so on, but when she was 1 month old it was time to crack on with work. Ben had his office downstairs in the only ground floor bedroom, and I moved a desk and chair into our spare bedroom upstairs for my office. Léna spent months 2 and 3 of her life on a folded blanket on the tiled floor of that room, looking up at an arc of toys, as I worked away next to her on my computer. Ben and I would communicate via Skype messages and from time to time I would take a break to breastfeed Léna before getting right back to it.

The pressure was on. We had to make this business work as otherwise we would end up losing our forever home, and moving back in with my mum and dad in the UK, and I really didn't want that. The stress of getting our business off the ground was certainly a contributing factor to my postnatal depression.

What we hadn't known then, which hindsight would have helped us with, was that a global recession was coming and that all spending in the luxury and the travel sectors would be cut right back, with big, long-standing companies going under.

We had no idea that our tiny, new business didn't stand a chance. We had no idea that we would close our business down just two years after opening it with such incredible dreams, excitement and motivation. We had no idea that we would sell our forever home to buy us some options. We had no idea that we would nearly pay the price of our marriage. We had no idea that trying to find work afterwards would be almost impossible. We had no idea that we would end up having to use our back-up plan of moving in with my parents - my 'worst case scenario' which I never thought we'd have to resort to. Despite all this we have no regrets about setting up and then closing down our first business. As I have learnt since - failure is an incredible teacher.

Task - how to know what the right decision is

Ben and I spent the good part of a year agonising over chucking in our stable, well-paid jobs to go into the unknown and set up our first business together. At least once a day I would moan to Ben that I "just wish I knew what the **right** decision is". I was 30 years old and hadn't had to make too many big, critical decisions up to that stage. And it was vital to me that I didn't take the **wrong** path. I was obsessed with there being one right decision and one wrong, like on those old TV game shows where you have a stack of money behind one door and a banana behind the other. For me it was black or white, right or wrong, succeed or fail. But which was which?

What I didn't realise - and wish someone had told me - back then was that there is NO right or wrong decision. They are just two different paths, two different options. And that you have no idea what is going to happen externally that might affect your decision. Maybe you take the great new job and the company goes bust. Maybe you buy that fab house and a new motorway gets built next to it. There will always be factors outside of your control.

Ben and I decided to set up a new business, we'd thought of all the ins and outs. What we hadn't prepped for was a global recession which would hit the luxury and the travel industries - both of which we were working with. So was it the wrong decision? No. It just took us on another, different path. Which through various twists and turns, via

Nice and London, over a period of 8 and a bit years, brought us to a life neither of us dreamt was possible here in Mauritius.

We would never have had this incredible life if our first business had worked out. So was it the wrong decision? I don't think so!

You want to know what the right decision is? Well let's take the pressure off right away as I explain to you that they are all the right decision. Now that stress is out of the way let's look at which one is the best for you right now.

Question number 1: what does your gut say? Answer the question without thinking and what is your answer?

Question number 2: if you never did this thing you are considering how would you feel?

Question number 3: what is the absolute worst case scenario if you do this thing? For us it was losing our dream home and moving back in with my parents. I thought it was the worst thing in the world, but in the end it was nowhere near as bad as in my head.

Question number 4: what is the absolute worst case scenario if you DON'T do this thing? For me it was staying in a job that I was no longer passionate about and wondering "what if?" as my life passed me by.

Question number 5: what is the absolute best case scenario if you do this thing? What COULD this mean for you? Versus what is the absolute best case scenario if you DON'T do this thing?

This is just the start of working out what the right decision is, there is a lot more to it than this, but if you want the basics remember these two things - there is no wrong decision, and listen to your gut.

(If you want to go further on decision-making there is a whole module on this in Life Reboot Camp.)

The one where I worked for a witch

I quickly realised, as the global recession slowly began to engulf France, that my CV was not very attractive there. With LE BROZEC closed down it was time to look for a job, but French employers like things to be nice and neat and linear, and to make perfect sense. My CV was anything but. And in a country where the university you went to, the degree you studied, and the year you graduated can still determine your starting salary for a job in your 40s, I was not a hot candidate.

The perfect French CV at the time looked something like this: good degree from a reputable university > masters' degree also from a reputable university > great starting job at a great company > promotion to a slightly better job at same company > promotion to yet another slightly better job at same company....forever until you retire.

My CV, on the other hand, resembled this: foreign language degree from a so-so university (AKA world's shittiest degree in France) > 6 months working as a trilingual secretary in a company that you can't really find information about > 2 ½ years working as an English language teacher in businesses > 4 months working as a bilingual PA in an international company > 3 ½ years working as a global PR manager in the same company (which made no sense to them as I had no degree or masters in marketing or PR to enable such a promotion to take place!) > 2 years running a luxury travel agency (what the what?!? Entrepreneurship? And in a totally different field from anything done before?!?).

My CV set off alarm bells, red flags, sniffer dogs and all sorts. No one wanted to touch me with a barge pole. France likes qualifications and grades and good schools and universities - if you jump through those hoops in your early 20s then you are set for life work-wise. If you have a patchwork CV like me then your hopes of finding work are very low.

I applied for anything and everything - PR work, marketing work, language work, even secretarial work again. But nobody liked the look of my CV. Until one day when I got invited to an interview for a marketing job at a film company. It was all very strange. The interview was with a woman in a cafe in a small village in the hinterland behind Nice. My potential future employer sounded very keen on the phone, the interview was in English and she had an accent that I couldn't place.

With butterflies in my stomach I drove the winding roads that took me to *St Jeannet* the next day, and had the most bizarre interview of my life. Jemma came across as quite eccentric, but after the closed ways of the French and their antiquated system of employing people this came as light relief. She excitedly told me about her company and the project she was working on, something to do with films, a website and a big launch party during the Cannes Film Festival a few weeks later.

It was very unclear what she did or what I was supposed to be doing but she offered me a job so I didn't really care at that stage, as long as it wasn't prostitution. The salary she was offering was ok too, until right at the end of the interview when she dropped a minor bombshell. She wouldn't actually be employing me. I needed to get myself set up as an *auto-entrepreneur* (a sole trader / freelancer) and she would contract me to work for her for 40 hours a week, like an employee. The contract she gave me to take home was super strict - what hours I should work, where that work should take place etc, however I was essentially a freelancer, with all the risks of freelancing: no holiday allowance, no sick pay etc.

Despite it not sounding great I was caught up in Jemma's excitement, and desperate to work, to bring in money and to get back on my feet again. A week later I met Jemma in a car park near her home (mansion) and followed her there in my car, as that's where I would be working 2-3 days a week, with the rest of the time spent working from home, and having Skype calls with Jemma whenever she so desired it.

She was very secretive about the work we were doing and who was onboard. We were planning this great, no expense spared, launch at the Majestic Hotel during the Cannes Film Festival and until I arrived I didn't know who was going to be there. She kept talking about George Clooney like he was a great friend of hers; as this was the French Riviera, she lived in a mansion, and was hosting a big party at the Majestic DURING the film festival, who knew what was possible?!?

Funnily enough there were no A-listers there, not even many Z-listers, but it was fun. I got to have my hair and make-up done for me, Ben was invited too and we got dressed up in our glad rags, drank champagne, ate delicious finger buffet food and got to hang out at the Majestic Hotel during Cannes' biggest time of the year.

Shortly after the festival I remember Jemma Skyping me one day when I was working from home. I'd set up a Twitter account for the company and she'd got me to follow various celebs including Matt

Damon. Ben was in the same room as me when she called and we both had to try not to burst out laughing as she instructed me to tweet Matt Damon.

"Just say to him - hi Matt, don't you think it's time to send the elevator back? Let's get in touch - he will see it and reply to us."

In all fairness this was in the early(ish) days of Twitter, it was 2009, but still I knew that this wasn't how Twitter worked, and we weren't suddenly going to become best buds with Matt Damon. I tried to explain to her that a) it was unlikely Matt Damon would see our tweet and b) even more unlikely that he would respond, but she wasn't having any of it. So that's how I spent one afternoon, tweeting celeb after celeb for my work.

I still didn't really understand what the company was supposed to be doing, but that didn't seem to worry Jemma unduly, which is strange when you think that I was the only person doing her marketing!

First of all I found Jemma to be quite funny and quirky, she was blonde and acted like a bimbo, but I realised later that this was very much put on. She knew exactly what she was doing, and was very good at getting her own way.

During my job interview Jemma explained to me that the reason she had come to live in this small French village, despite being from the Balkans originally, was because she was a witch. And in a past life she had been burnt at the stake in this sleepy hillside village. At that stage I didn't care what she thought, I just wanted a job, any job. But as time went on these quirks got harder to deal with.

On the 2-3 days a week that I worked with Jemma in her home I sat opposite her, perched on an armchair, facing her as she smoked cigarette after cigarette, with my computer balanced on my lap, for 8 hours a day. My lunch 'break' was also spent opposite her, across a table this time, eating the food that her maid had made for us. It was always some kind of salad as she was watching her weight. She would dish up my lunch and when my plate was half-full (of veggies) she would say to me "that's enough for you!".

I couldn't take food of my own to her house and I ate whatever and however much Jemma decided / dictated I would eat. Within 2 months of working for her I lost 4kg (nearly 9 pounds) and it's not like I was big to start with.

The only time I got a break from her was when I went to the toilet. The rest of the day was spent breathing in secondhand smoke, trying to stretch out my back from the uncomfortable sitting position in the armchair, and answering any weird and wonderful questions she cared to fire at me.

One day Jemma excitedly told me that she had found a cure for cancer, a statement to which I wasn't expected to object or question. She excitedly explained to me that she had found the cure for cancer but she couldn't share it with anyone otherwise the illuminati were going to come for her. As she explained all this to me I had to respond appropriately i.e. not crack up laughing or ask incredulously WTF? But to look interested and to be all "wow, really? How amazing!".

The cancer cure - or what I could grasp of it - was to eat the insides of fruits with stones and pips. Jemma explained to me if I ate the pips of apples, the small "pip" inside peach stones and other such fruits then I wouldn't get cancer and it would cure people who did have the disease.

As she told me this it just so happened that she had some apples in the house, she gave me one to eat and told me "you have to eat the whole thing, pips and all, and don't try to throw it in the bin as I will check there!".

It is possibly one of the weirdest working environments I've ever been in. Within 3 months of working there I was losing my mind. I honestly thought I was going to go crazy, and that was just spending 2-3 days with her a week. I knew I needed a way out but I also knew how hard it was for me to find work in France, luckily I did manage to escape and less than a year later things changed drastically for us...

The one where we chose to become jobless and homeless

You really can't beat London in the sunshine and warmth. There really isn't a happier, high energy place anywhere on the planet. Everyone spills out of pubs into beer gardens, frisbees are thrown in parks across the city, the smell of barbecues permeates the air, bikinis come out, t-shirts come off and laughter and smiles abound. You can't help but be sucked in.

In April 2010 Ben, Léna and I boarded a plane for London to attend my sister's wedding. It wasn't gloriously hot and sunny, and it wasn't that warm even (certainly not in comparison to the French Riviera). But the sun did shine and people seemed happier than Nice, there was an air of promise, Nice seemed grey in comparison.

A day spent in the company of my family (direct and extended) brought on the biggest feeling of homesickness that I'd ever felt, before or since. Ben had been asking me for months (years?) to move to London. He had previously lived and worked in San Francisco and loved the Anglo-Saxon way of doing things, far preferring it to the French way. In addition Léna was 3 years old and French was very much her dominant language, if I didn't forbid it she would speak to me in her father's tongue too. She even had a French accent when speaking English, despite only ever hearing English from native speakers.

Was now the right time to move? I'd always vowed I would live in France for the rest of my life and that I would never return to the UK to live. I loved it there (didn't I?). But was I enforcing restrictions on myself that were cutting me off from opportunities? After having to close our luxury travel agency business down neither Ben nor I were exactly fulfilled in our work, in fact that was the understatement of the century. But England? Really? I'd lived in France since graduating from university in 1998. I'd lived my whole adult life in France. I'd bought and sold two houses there, figured out car troubles, DIY, pregnancy, childbirth and child-rearing there. My friends were there. We lived a stone's throw from the beach in Nice.

But I knew Ben really hated his job and really wanted to move to London. How would I feel if the shoe was on the other foot and he didn't make that effort for me?

It was just a random Friday in June 2010 when Ben called me from work to say that things were going from bad to worse. His mental health had been heading southwards since he'd taken this current job, and I could hear in his voice that the situation couldn't last.

"Just get through today" I told him "I will have a solution when you get home, I promise".

Immediately after hanging up the phone I dialled my parents' number.

"Hi Mum! Please can Ben, Léna and I move in with you indefinitely?" I greeted my mum with.

I knew that I had to do whatever it took to get my husband out of this hole of despair that he'd landed in, and I knew how much London meant to him. Marriage is all about for better and for worse, in sickness and in health, I needed to help Ben with his worse.

That evening, with my parents' OK ringing in my head, I sat Ben down at the dining room table and told him we were selling up, downsizing and moving in with my parents, until we could find jobs and a place to live in London. At first he was reluctant, he knew how much Nice and France meant to me, but I told him it was a non-negotiable, it was what he needed and wanted, so we would give it a try.

We made our decision that night, choosing to become jobless and homeless, and exactly one month and one day later we boarded a flight for London. I moved back in to my childhood home, aged 34, accompanied by my husband and our 3 year old daughter. I was too drained by the stress and to do list from the move to be able to process the move or what it meant, the emotions would come later, in a big way.

Task - how to find a way out when there is no way out

After deciding to close LE BROZEC down with the global recession crushing companies in its path things were hard. Finding work was incredibly difficult for both Ben and me, but it felt like there was no way out. The recession was affecting everyone, companies were closing down, jobs were fewer on the ground and our CVs were not popular in France. In the country where the word *entrepreneur* comes from they are not big fans of these risk-takers. It felt like there was no way out. There seemed to be no end in sight to the recession and shortage of jobs in our area. So I took a step back and took geography out of the question.

My parents live in Berkshire, about one hour outside of London, where lots of big companies have their UK or even European head offices, so I had always found well-paid jobs easily there. I knew that London would be even better for job-hunting. However I had to deal with all the emotions around this. I had lived in France for 12 years. All my good friends were there. I WORSHIPPED the sun and needed the warmth to survive. I also felt more French than English most of the time. I'd left the UK aged 22 so had done all my adulting in France. Could I leave this country that I had fallen in love with 26 years previously? The place I'd always said I'd never leave.

Sometimes the way out can be a painful one. Often when there seems to be no solution there is one, but it won't be easy or without sacrifice.

And you need to remember this if you are struggling to find your own way out right now. It might be hidden. It might not be obvious. It might seem crazy.

Strip your life back to the absolute basics and then build back on from there to see what options you have.

For example when we were miserable in France I could have stripped my life back like this:

- Whatever solution I go for HAS to include Ben and Léna.
- We need a roof over our head and food to eat.
- At least one of us needs a paid job.
- Ideally I would like to take our dog and cat with us, but if that is not possible then I will make peace with it.

Now that is really stripping things back. But when you look at it like this you realise that you have so many options. Ben has a degree in Maths and a masters in IT. I have a degree in French and Spanish. We both speak fluent English and French. We both had a range of experience, including working internationally. We both had European Union passports so had a whole host of countries open to us.

Once you take out the emotions of "but this is my home and I don't want to leave" you realise just how many options you have.

This is just one example around work and moving. No matter where or how you are stuck there is always a way out. Just strip your life back to the basics that you can't live without and see what your options are.

If you'd like to access all the tasks in this book more easily go and grab the free book bonuses over here: www.SophieLeBrozec.com/happy-bonus amongst other bonuses you'll get a PDF grouping all the tasks together in one document, so you can quickly and easily work through them.

The one where we moved to London

I was lying on our sofa bed in the boot of our Peugeot Partner, holding on to the tailgate with all my might as Ben drove round bends in Nice. It was our last day in Nice, we had about 10 hours before our flight left and in that time we had to deliver the bed we'd just slept on to Léna's old childminder, hand over our car to its new owner, empty the rest of our apartment and catch a bus to the airport with one suitcase and carry-on each.

Léna's old childminder lived nearby so it hadn't seemed so crazy to drive the sofa bed to her, until we realised we couldn't close the boot of the car, and had nothing to hold it in place...other than my hand. We made it to her place, safe and sound, without me or the sofa bed flying out of the car. Once we'd helped carry it up to her apartment we could tick that off the list.

Next it was time to take our bins out and put them on the street outside our apartment. There was A LOT as we emptied the fridge and kitchen cupboards. And they looked quite conspicuous in the middle of the day on the street in a nice area of central Nice. Within half an hour of putting them outside our buzzer rang, it was the local police asking us to go downstairs.

Were these our bin bags and was this our rubbish? Errrrr, I couldn't lie, they'd opened up a bin bag and found an old envelope in it leading them, sleuth-like to ring on our buzzer. Crap! They were telling us we had to take them all the way to the rubbish dump, but we just didn't have time.

Ben loaded them up into the car (which we'd had cleaned for the new owner!), drove around the corner and dumped them by big restaurant bins that would be emptied that evening. I'm not proud of our actions but we were up against the clock and our stress levels were off the charts.

An hour later it was time to deliver our car to its new owner, and we were almost ready to go. We had time for one last dip in the sea before a quick shower and the big off.

It was bittersweet swimming in the sea that last day. We'd gone for a dip at midnight the night before, with 3 year old Léna as nobody could sleep due to the heat, but this was our farewell swim. I knew that London was the right next step for us but saying goodbye to Nice was so hard. I couldn't allow myself to think of it right then. There were 12 consecutive years of living in the area to process, not to mention the two times I lived in Nice previously as a student. I had too much I needed to DO before I could THINK about all of this. Looking around and seeing tourists on the beach, delighted with their sunny beach holiday I had a moment of panic - why were we walking away from all this?! Most people would give anything to live in a beautiful big apartment a stone's throw from the beach in Nice, and we were walking away from it all. To move back into my childhood home. In a town I couldn't leave fast enough.

I swallowed down the lump in my throat that risked turning into hysteria if I gave in to it. We left Léna in her (completely empty and void of all furniture) bedroom while we quickly showered and packed up our last bits and pieces. When it was time to get her dressed I went into her room and the tears that I was desperately holding in nearly broke free. Léna was lying asleep on the bare wooden floor of her bedroom, her thumb in her mouth, her *doudou* in her hand. She reminded me of pictures of street children, asleep on the streets with nothing but an old cuddly toy. What the fuck were we about to put our baby through?!? Taking her away from everything and everyone she knew.

I literally shook my head to clear all "what if?" thoughts and to push on with the agenda. Next on the list - dress Léna. After that - walk to bus stop. Then - get on plane, fly to London, get met by parents, go to bed in my childhood home and figure out life tomorrow.

The next bit all went smoothly and I woke up at my mum and dad's the next morning feeling happy with the 20°C after the 35°C that we'd been experiencing in Nice. We decided to give ourselves a week's holiday upon our arrival in the UK as the last month in Nice had been so manic. It was such a pleasure to see my parents again; even after 12 years of living abroad I never got over how much I missed being away from them. And to this day I still maintain that the hardest part of being an expat is being far from family, my parents in particular.

We quickly got over our excitement at the cooler temperatures as the sun battled to show its face and the thermometer hovered just below the 20°C mark. The novelty very quickly wore off and within 2 weeks of our arrival Ben announced that it was the longest he'd gone in his 34 year life without seeing the sun. I told him "you'd better get used to it as it's summer!".

The move was hard on everyone. We had had to leave our beloved dog and cat behind in France for 6 months as we waited for all their paperwork to be in place before they could travel. Léna was bored and got under our feet - in Nice she had pre-school and during the holidays she had holiday club, and she loved spending her days there, playing with the other kids.

I quickly discovered that there are far fewer childcare options in the UK and that they were a hell of a lot more expensive. In France most mums go back to work, at least 4 days a week, so there is an abundance of childcare which is so affordable, especially as what you pay is based on your income.

On the plus side Ben found a fantastic job within one week of looking, not only was it interesting but it was also twice his Nice salary, and within 6 months of us arriving in the UK he had tripled his French income.

With Ben's job guaranteed we could start house-hunting, now we knew where he would be working. We narrowed down the location to Balham and Clapham in southwest London as my brother Tim lived in Balham, plus my cousin Becky and a good friend from university lived in Clapham. They were also both really accessible for my parents.

We had what we felt was a pretty good budget and set up three house / flat viewings. The first one nearly had me on a flight back to Nice. It was an ex-council flat on a main road in Clapham, so I didn't expect a palace but I knew some were really nice. As we walked around the place we realised this wasn't one of them. The estate agent tried to brush off the mould I pointed out to him as "just needing a good clean". Everything was dirty, broken or unsafe. As we left the building to head off to our next visit we watched a man fall down, as he passed out, dead drunk. We asked the estate agent what the building was he'd just come out of, he looked sheepish as he mentioned it was some kind of a halfway house.

Now I'm not overly precious in general, I mean in Nice we had a prostitute on the corner of our street every evening who Léna would wave to, and that didn't bother me at all. But this man was just the last straw on a whole pile of shit.

I turned to Ben and asked him (slightly hysterically) in French "what the fuck are we doing?!". Which is out of character, as I am usually the one to find the silver lining somewhere even on thick, black clouds.

He urged me not to make any rash decisions until we'd seen the other places. The next one was another ex-council flat, but this one was the first floor of a high rise of flats, surrounded by other high rise flats. The bedrooms were the size of cupboards and the 'view' from the windows was of the other high rises.

What had we done? We had left a (slight) sea view of the Mediterranean in a beautiful, enormous, high-ceilinged period apartment in Nice for fuck's sake!

We had one place left to visit before getting the train back to my mum and dad's house and Léna who they'd been looking after all day. Were we going to leave London as failures?

The last place was a house and just one road down from Tim's flat, plus it had Tooting Common at the end of the road, which looked great for walking our dog when he finally arrived in the country.

I tried to keep my hopes high and my mind open, but I was in total panic under the surface, just about keeping it together for Ben who was so excited to be in London, and so delighted about his new job. I owed it to him and to Léna to do this properly and give it a shot.

The last place was a Victorian terraced house with bay windows in the lounge and a long narrow corridor. We had barely made it to the foot of the stairs, 5 steps into the house, before I turned to Ben and said in French, "it's good, we can take this one". As we visited the rest of the house we didn't clock the revolting decorations or mismatched furniture, all we could see was that this was a house we could live in as a family, somewhere we could raise our daughter, and possibly have more children.

One month later we waved goodbye to my parents and moved in to our new home. London Baby! On the day we moved in the doorbell rang, I opened it to Tim who announced

"45 seconds. It's just taken me 45 seconds to walk from my flat to your house."

That boded well as we both got on well with Tim and I had missed my family so much whilst living in France.

Over a beer I asked my child-free brother if he knew if there was a decent school nearby. I knew this made me a freak of nature in the UK. I had a daughter who was 3 years and 10 months old and had just signed a year-long lease for a house without even looking into the schools in the area.

Tim burst out laughing and informed me that we had one of the best schools in the area at the end of our road (the other end from the Common), that people fiddled their addresses and moved houses to be able to get their kids in there. Finally it seemed as if things were looking up. But looks can be deceptive.

After desperately wanting to be a SAHM (stay at home mum) when Léna was a baby I had finally got used to being a working mum. I liked earning my own money, having independence and spending my time with adults. But in the UK we only had part-time childcare for Léna; she didn't have a place at the local nursery school as her name had only just gone on the list. We had found an au pair who had moved in with us but she was only allowed to work a certain number of hours a week, certainly not enough to cover me working a full-time job plus commuting time.

So I found myself spending time with Léna just the two of us as I sank into some kind of mild depression. My fur babies were still in France. Léna was looking to me for entertainment after being used to days full of other kids and fun activities. Ben was at work. Anyone I knew in London was at work. I didn't know any other local mums. It was cold, grey and miserable, and it was only October. In Nice this was still beach time. I felt lonely and sad. I missed Nice and my friends there so much. I missed adult company. I missed feeling like I had some kind of worth. And I couldn't tell anyone. Who can complain when they're not working and just have to look after their nearly 4 year old daughter? Those aren't real problems. And I didn't want to worry anyone. Especially not Ben who was really enjoying his new job. So I took a slightly drastic measure…

The enormity of what we had done hit me hard. I'd made this grand gesture about doing this for Ben as he was so unhappy in Nice, but what about if the flip side of the coin meant I was so unhappy in London? Were we both allowed happiness at the same time and in the same place?

I really missed having our pets around, and I started to go onto cat shelter websites and Battersea dog and cat home's website. I knew our dog and cat would be joining us in London in just a few months but I needed fur, I needed animal love. I was so lonely.

Ben must have sensed how badly I was doing as he gave in to my request to adopt two black kittens. Black because we used to have a cat in France who was hit by a car when I was pregnant with Léna; two because I didn't want one to feel lonely; kittens because there were two black kittens that needed a home and what is cuter than kittens?!

The day they entered our home, hearts and lives was a turning point for me. Whilst they were a pain in the arse (like human babies, dog babies and most other animal babies, cat babies look cute but cause a lot of trouble) with their running all over the furniture, scaling curtains and playing all night, they stopped me feeling so lonely. I would sit with them on my lap, stroking them and just generally feeling so much better.

The grey cloud that had been parked over my head more or less since we arrived back in the UK started to dissipate. Léna got a nursery place at the local school, it was only half days (a joke after her 8am-6pm in France) but it was better than nothing, and so good for both of us. This meant I could seriously look for work, as our au pair could look after Léna around the nursery hours.

Within a week of Léna starting nursery I got a phone call from a recruitment agency who had found my CV online. Was I available and could I go for an interview the next day? That would be a yes, and a hell yes! Within a week I had had two interviews with the company in question, accepted their job offer and started work. Just a tiny bit different after all the hoop jumping I'd had to do to get a job in France!

Life suddenly got so much better. I was working in a small office in central London, within easy walking distance of the London Eye, St Paul's Cathedral and the Shard (as it was being built). I was earning my own money. I was spending time with (lovely) adults. I was using my brain and it was interesting. I felt like I was Ben's equal again. I started to think that London wasn't such a bad idea after all.

The one where I got accused of child abuse

It was May 2011, but I remember it as clearly as if it were yesterday. I know exactly where I was when the phone call came, and I remember every single word.

"Léna has had a fall, and she's ok, but it's her arm...we're waiting for an ambulance."

These words came down the phone to me, and I couldn't really take it in.

One minute I was at work, and the next minute I was awash with Mummy Guilt as I realised my 4 year old was hurt. And I wasn't there. Not even close. Some would say that is the price you pay for working in central London.

I rushed back to my desk, still holding it together, as I told my boss I had to go to the hospital, that my daughter was hurt.

I rang Ben and told him to meet me at St George's. I made it to the end of that call before the racking sobs came. I'd let her down. I'd let my baby down. I hadn't been there for her when she'd needed me. I'd been too busy furthering my career, and thinking of myself. Not her.

As I rushed to the tube station I rang my mum and cried down the phone to her.

"Léna's fallen...she's hurt...her arm...I don't know." Not making sense as I attempted to talk through the tears.

My mum did her best to reassure me that Léna would be fine, that kids fall all the time and break their arms and legs. But I was convinced it was worse. Little did I know…

We'd only been back in the UK for 10 months and in London for 8 of those months. So I didn't even know how to get to the hospital. I got in a cab as I left the tube station in Tooting, not knowing I was just around the corner.

As I arrived at St George's (the place that would hold happier memories as we welcomed Clémence into the world there 18 months later) I ran around wildly, looking for A & E (Accident & Emergency), and for my baby.

I found her, with Ben, and two doctors. Relief flooded me as she seemed ok.

But I was quickly taken to one side by a doctor who explained the extent of her injury. She seemed ok because she was dosed up on morphine. My 4 year old baby! On such hardcore drugs!

It turned out that she hadn't had a standard childhood break, but had fractured her humerus bone, which would require more intensive surgery.

It was too late in the day for them to operate so they booked her in for the next morning. What I wasn't told was that the morphine would wear off and I would spend the night listening to my daughter screaming, in a way I had only heard before in the torture scenes of the TV series, *24*.

That was the longest night of my life. Followed by the longest morning of my life as Léna underwent 4 hours of surgery, involving a neurologist and a plastic surgeon. They ended up having to cut open her arm as the broken bone was pressing on an artery and a nerve. When she was finally out of surgery I heaved a sigh of relief....only to be told that she needed to spend the next 24 hours in intensive care as it had been such a serious break followed by such intensive surgery.

Whilst trying to get my head around all this in intensive care - she was under a heated blanket and hooked up to a catheter - a doctor came and took me to one side.

"So how exactly did your 4 year old daughter manage to break her humerus?" he started, no beating around the bush.

Luckily I knew exactly what was going on. They were - quite rightly - checking for child abuse. Upon our arrival at the hospital the day before, we had called my mother-in-law, who is a doctor, to tell her what had happened, and she was shocked to hear that a 4 year old, of Léna's tiny frame, had managed to break her humerus with just her own weight. It turns out that you need to whack it with something seriously hard to break it, and the weight of a tiny 4 year old would not have been enough. Which is why the doctor wanted to know how on earth this had happened.

After the discussion with my mother-in-law we had asked more questions about what had happened at the local playground. It turns out Léna had been climbing a play tractor, had lost her grip and fallen, hitting a metal bar on the way down to the spongy floor below.

I was able to explain all this to the doctor, along with the fact that I was at work at the time, and we were off the hook, but it did scare me about how easily an accident could look like child abuse. Although of course I am encouraged that the staff were following through on this risk.

Léna and I ended up staying in hospital for 4 nights before we were finally able to go home, with Léna sporting a plaster cast so heavy she had to support it with her other arm. To this day she still has the surgery scar, which grows with her and now measures an impressive 16cm on her 12 year old arm.

    After the event we were encouraged by other local parents to report the accident to the council who manage the playground as there had been other - not quite as serious - accidents there. I filed a report, but didn't want to press charges, and within a few months the playground had been razed to the ground and a completely different style built in its place. So at least I feel like I saved someone else's family from this heartache.

Task - how to deal with Mummy Guilt

Do you know what? There wasn't one second that Ben questioned himself with regard to Léna's accident, he didn't question his parenting decisions or the fact he was at work when it happened. He didn't feel an ounce of guilt (and he's quite a sensitive soul).

For him, the father, it was just one of those things that happen.

Kids play and sometimes get hurt.

For me it was a clear sign that I was a bad mum. It was quite obviously my fault. I shouldn't have been at work. I was clearly selfish and putting myself before my child so wasn't fit to parent.

I should have been with her.

I should have provided better childcare for her.

No matter which way I looked at it I was to blame, at fault, in the wrong, and the guilt nearly crippled me.

Fast-forward a good few years and I'm older (definitely) and wiser (to a certain extent, but still learning).

I KNOW that a happy mum, doing what fulfils her, is a far better mum than one doing what she feels she 'should' be doing.

I KNOW that I wasn't to blame, and that there was no guilt to apportion. It was just one of those things.

These days I am mostly guilt-free. I am a good mum but sometimes bad things happen. I know that if I do the best I can, at that given time, then there is no guilt to be passed around.

As I finalise this book, ready to be published, I'm in the UK for 3 weeks, without my girls, who are in Mauritius with Ben, and I feel absolutely zero guilt about not being with them. However it has taken a while to get to this stage.

Us mums are the absolute queens of the guilt-trip. We beat ourselves up because we forgot the bake sale at school. We vow never to forgive ourselves when our youngest gets sick during a child-free night out.

If we are working mums we feel guilty as we say goodbye to sleepy little ones who don't really understand why we're not taking them to school.

Us work at home mums get a dose of the guilts as we put the kids in front of the TV as we rush to meet a deadline.

And the stay at home mums amongst us feel guilty about dreaming of being elsewhere than with our children. Guilty about wanting more or different. Guilty about being bored with our kids. Guilty about not contributing financially to the family.

Since my arrival into the world of parenting in late 2006 I've turned my hand to all of the aforementioned roles, and felt guilty in all of them. It doesn't matter how you juggle your life as a mum, guilt tends to play a starring role.

But it doesn't have to be that way. You can calm that guilt voice right down, and even sometimes shut it up completely.

Grab a pen and paper and spend some time working out where you are at with guilt in your life.

What guilt are you carrying around with you? Something you've been beating yourself up over for years? Or a more recent event? It could well be more than one specific thing, or it might be a general feeling.

Take a step back and ask yourself if a man or a dad in the same situation would be feeling guilt. Us women, and us mums in particular, are world class in our ability to feel guilt.

Write down the facts of the event / incident and ask yourself, or a close friend, if this is really something to feel guilty about.

If it's just a general feeling then write down when the feeling comes, is it when someone makes a comment, or when you are looking at other people's lives on social media? What sparks this feeling of guilt?

Again ask yourself, or a close friend, if this is just a story you're telling yourself, or if it's really something to feel guilty about.

Moving forward next time you feel guilt, ask yourself these questions:

1. Did anyone get hurt (physically or emotionally)?
2. Is anyone else involved feeling guilty? Your partner? A school teacher? A grandparent? Your child?
3. Is someone making you feel guilty? Or are you doing that job yourself?
4. Will it matter tomorrow? Next week? Next month? Next year? Next decade? How big of a deal is it really? Léna's broken arm happened in 2011, but her scar grows with her and will be with her for life. It would be easy to beat myself up for this for the rest of my days. But I now refuse to do that. Shit happens. She is fine and healthy and it doesn't stop her doing anything. So please don't beat yourself up.

Can you reframe it or turn it around? Can you laugh with your child about it? Can you share it as a funny story on social media or at a dinner party? Being able to laugh at yourself removes so much of the pressure.

Lastly, remember that most of us are just doing the best we can at any given time. You included. So go easy on yourself.

Get all the tasks from this book in one easy-to-access PDF, head over here to download it: www.SophieLeBrozec.com/happy-bonus

The one(s) where I wanted to eBay Léna

It was 8.50am on a Friday morning in October in London, the weather had started to get cold which pissed me off as I hate the cold and I could no longer fit my winter coat around my 8 month pregnant belly. I was fed up of being pregnant and was so ready for it to be over and to meet our new baby.

"Léna!" I yelled up the stairs to the nearly 6 year old who was trying my patience more and more every day, "it's nearly time to go! Are you ready?"

"I can't find the blue thing for Show & Tell," came the reply.

Oh crap. Trying to find a non-descriptive object 8 minutes before we needed to leave the house for school was so not what I needed right now.

I lumbered my heavy body up the stairs to Léna's bedroom, wracking my brains for what the blue thing could be. Léna is a hoarder of all things bright and beautiful, all creatures great and small, but also all things ugly and dull so this could have been literally anything.

"We're leaving in 5 minutes so get whatever it is you need for Show & Tell and let's go, go, go!" I clapped my hands on the 'go's to drum home that time was of the essence. But she was having none of it.

"It's the blue thing that Daddy brought home for me," was the only additional description I got to help me find the indeterminate object.

Daddy had been on a business trip abroad recently, bringing home with him a myriad of weird and wonderful gifts, including Léna's 'blue thing' which really could have been anything. I certainly didn't have the time or the patience to figure out what the hell it could be.

"You don't have time to find it now, you can look for it this weekend and take it in on Monday. We are leaving in 2 minutes so you either find something else for Show & Tell or you go without today."

Apparently these were not the words that Léna wanted to hear as she went into full-on meltdown mode. All I could think as I watched this child of mine howl, and writhe in some kind of agony on the floor was that I didn't really like her right now. Don't get me wrong, I loved her, but I didn't especially like her at this moment in time. She was constantly pushing my buttons and every day seemed to be edging me closer to the border of sanity. What the hell was I thinking considering doing all this again? My hand went to my swollen stomach as my unborn baby kicked, and I sighed at the prospect of going through all this with TWO kids.

I checked my watch. 8.57am. School started at 9am and whilst it was literally at the end of our road we were still cutting it really fine.

"We are going!" I announced in what I hoped was an authoritative, I've got everything under control, don't give me any crap, voice. Sadly the fact I was in charge seemed to go right over her head as she wailed "NOOOOOOOOOOOOO!"

For Fuck's Sake! Why don't people warn you when you buy all those baby books, that it's not books on learning how to deal with babies that you need, it's books about how not to throttle your 5 year old?

Then all of a sudden, as I was pulling on my coat and taking Léna's to her, I realised not only what the blue thing was, but also where it was. It was some sort of blue evil eye stone thing, I found it, thrust it into Léna's hand as I pulled her and her school bag out of the door. Suddenly she was all sweetness and light as she skipped down the road.

We speed-walked / ran (the running bit was Léna, not me) the 100 metres to the school gate and stepped inside just as the bell rang. I was so over Léna's behaviour. I was so over fricking Show & Tell every fricking day. I was so over being pregnant. And Léna's poor 20-something year old teacher, fresh out of her teacher training programme, learnt all that at 9am that Friday morning.

"Miss Page! Stop with the Show & Tell! I can't take it anymore, it's 9am and I already need vodka and I can't because I'm pregnant, just STOP ok?" I ranted hysterically.

Later that day a letter came home from school, informing all parents that from now on Show & Tell would only be on a Monday, and would only be to show something that the children had got from a recent trip or outing, to avoid the large number of random Show & Tells that were coming in to school.

I felt like a bitch for raging at Léna's very nice teacher, and at my young child, but I did also feel like I scored a small victory for all parents at the school that day.

It didn't matter what I said or did to Léna, she would not listen to me; she ran on her own time, tidied up when it suited her, ate how and how much she wanted, and basically didn't give a shit that I was her mum, and that she was supposed to listen to, and obey, me. Whilst I was excited about being on early maternity leave and home with my big girl for the last few months of my pregnancy, I kept thinking how much I was lacking as a mum.

One evening I even joked to Ben that we should probably think about eBaying Léna, that's how hard she was to handle at the time. I couldn't get her to listen to me ever. Let alone actually do what I wanted her to do. She was so strong-willed and it was driving me mad. One day when my mum was over I ranted to her about it, to which my mum raised her eyebrows, looked pointedly at me and said "oh yeah, I know all about strong-willed daughters!". Point taken. So I was strong-willed too, and this was just karma, but what could I do about it?

As Mum said, it was a good thing to have strong daughters, as you know they will do great things and won't let themselves be walked over. But oh dear God! Could they not just be feisty once they were out in the world as adults, and leave off practising it at home?!

Eventually it was Ben who found a way to let Léna know we were in charge, as we were both at the end of our tether with not being able to discipline her. Nothing worked. If we told her there was no TV for her she simply replied, all teenage attitude aged 5, "don't care!". If we told her she couldn't have any sweets, biscuits, treats etc it was the same shrug and "don't care!". If we told her to go to her room, sit on the naughty step, go to the corner it was the same, "don't care!".

Finally Ben snapped. Yet again Léna was refusing to do something simple we'd asked her to do, and was giving us the biggest teenage attitude about it. Ben told her "this is your last chance, do it now or I will go to your room, choose a toy and go and put it in the bin outside. Not the recycling bin, the big, dirty bin, and you'll never see it again!" Léna wavered but didn't cave, and Ben, true to his word, stormed into her room, grabbed one of the many cuddly toys in there (not a favourite), showed it to Léna and had her watch him throw it in the bin outside.

I nearly burst into tears. We were such evil parents. What was wrong with us? Why weren't we like all other parents, with perfect kids, who actually obeyed their mum and dad? Léna looked at Ben with such anger in her eyes, turned around and stormed off to her bedroom.

The next time we had to discipline her Ben tried it again, grabbing another toy from her room. Again Léna didn't cave and watched another toy disappear forever. I wondered what we were going to do with Léna, she had a will of iron. But it seemed this was getting through, as next time Ben threatened to throw out a toy Léna gave in. And from then on things shifted. She now knew we were in charge. It didn't mean she didn't push her luck, but she didn't want to lose any more toys, and so would always end up doing what we asked her to do. But bloody hell it was a tough lesson.

I'd heard of being cruel to be kind but I hadn't realised until I was a mum what it meant. I thought being a mum was going to be all about showering my child with love, hugs and kisses. After my miscarriage any child of mine was going to be doubly loved and wanted. I was going to be the perfect mum. I would be so close to my kids. I never realised just how tough or strict I would need to be. Just how hard I would have to be with my child.

As Léna's got older I've been able to explain things to her with a chance of her understanding, and I've told her

"I would LOVE to say yes to you on everything, that would make my life SO much easier. Yes you can have as many sweets as you want, yes you can watch what you want on TV for as long as you want, yes you can go to bed when you want," but that would make me such a bad mum."

As I've explained to her so many times, it is much harder to say no, but in general I am saying it because it is the right thing for her.

At the time of writing this Léna is 12 years old and people often ask me if I'm worried about the teenage years, but I joke with them that we've already been through the teenage years with Léna. She was born a teenager, from wanting to stay up and party with us from a baby then sleep late the next day, to giving us attitude, being sulky and refusing to do things; she gave us all the teenage crap from around 18 months old until about 8 or 9 years old. Then she started to mellow.

She has always been mature but in the last few years she has turned into this wonderful, empathic, caring, sensitive individual who understands others, children and adults alike, who can see when I need her help and gives it. In the last 2 years she has often said to me things like "you look tired, do you want me to put Clémence to bed?" and she excelled herself last year when she was 11 and I was solo parenting while Ben was in Europe.

It was going well and we were having a good time; as it was the school holidays Léna and I had got into a pattern of her doing the washing-up while I put Clémence to bed, before watching something on TV together in the evening. Then one evening, just after coming back downstairs, I was really ill, diarrhoea, vomiting, the works, out of nowhere. I finally crawled from the bathroom to the lounge, ghostly white, and told Léna,

"I'm sick, I've just been really ill".

She jumped into action,

"Do you want me to get you a sick bowl? Do you want a drink? Water? Something else? Some crackers?"

She was 11 years old and was running around after me, caring for me, like my own mum would have, and my mum is normally the only person I want to look after me when I'm sick, and yes, I do realise I'm a grown woman who still likes to be looked after by her mum! But Léna was an absolute trooper. And this seems to be the person that she has grown into. I feel like we've already been through the desert of the teenage years and now we are in the glory days of the 20s, of an age when we can be peers.

Léna shares so much with me and we talk so much about life, goals, hopes, dreams, likes, dislikes, everything. We still have a mother-daughter relationship, but it is an incredibly close one now. Something I never thought possible just 7 years ago when I was so ready to eBay her.

Task - how to like your child when you are really struggling to

I'm not proud of the period when I wanted to eBay Léna. She was hard. It was hard. Emotions ran high and there was no bloody manual telling us how to deal with that strong-willed madam. I was at the stage where I loved Léna but I really didn't like her. I would sometimes watch her sleep to remember those feelings of love, because during the day she drove me so mad. We joke about it now and Léna thinks it's hilarious what a nightmare she was and that I used to dream about eBaying her. But it was no joke at the time.

If you are in the trenches with this your kids here are some things I want to share with you.

- You are not alone. There are a gazillion of us out there going through this, it's just very few people raise their hands publicly to share it.
- Your child is not doing this to hurt you or out of spite. They are figuring things out. Trying to understand who they are, what the rules are. Working out how flexible your boundaries are. They are not evil. Even though some days it might seem like they are.
- Do not try to figure out how you will get through the weekend or the school holidays or that trip to Grandma's at Christmas. Just work on the here and now and what's going on today. Don't stress what is still to come.

- Look after YOU. This is emotionally challenging and exhausting. Find someone to lean on - your partner, a good friend, sister, mum, online support group - and share what you're going through, how you're struggling, how it makes you feel. Don't hold it in. And make sure you make time for you, to do things that recharge those batteries that your child is busy draining.
- Don't be afraid to ask for professional advice. There are a ton of people out there to help with children's behaviour, tantrums and all sorts. Do ask. Do get suggestions and ideas of things to try out.
- Remember YOU are the boss. No matter how hard that is to enforce, it is important that your child knows their place in the family / household hierarchy. Sometimes you have to be cruel to be kind, never more so than with kids.
- Be clear on boundaries. Make sure everyone knows what the rules are and keep them rigid. Children, especially younger ones, like the security of knowing where they stand. They might try to push the barriers a bit but really they want to know these walls are safe and will protect them.
- Know that what feels like hell now could well be dinner party talk in a few years, so try not to get sucked too low by it all.
- Try and spend some good one-to-one time with your child, fun stuff that you both like doing. Things that won't provoke tempers, tantrums or arguments (from either of you) so you can just enjoy being together.
- If you really struggle to be around your child keep the time you are together to small bursts, instead of drawn out sessions of

time in each other's pockets, when you are likely to drive each
other mad.

- When things are really hard, watch your child as they innocently
  and peacefully sleep and remember just how lovely they really
  are.

If you are feeling like you are at the end of your tether with your child /
children, and it's bringing you down, make sure you download the free
bonuses that go with this book, I think the checklist for how to be
happy will help you. You can access all the bonuses here:
www.SophieLeBrozec.com/happy-bonus

The one where I gave birth in 59 minutes

As we headed down Balham High Road, in the rush hour of a Monday morning, I caught my dad's eyes looking at me anxiously in the rear view mirror in between my contractions. Various thoughts went through my not-so-lucid mind as I saw southwest London go by. The first thing was "why is my dad looking anxious?" is it a) because his youngest daughter is mooing like a cow on the backseat of his car, and sounds like she's in pain, poor baby? Or b) (more likely) because he's only just bought this car and his youngest daughter's waters haven't broken yet, and it's a 20 minute drive to the hospital at this time of day.

The next thought was why on earth am I mooing? I'd heard about women mooing in labour, but I thought it was put on, it was certainly nothing I felt called to do when giving birth to Léna, but then I suppose that was a whole other ball game with my induction in France. Yet here I was, mooing like a cow, in the back of my dad's Ford Focus, half thinking I should stop as I sounded like a loon, but actually realising that I couldn't even if I wanted to.

In the same vein I couldn't stop barking at my mum in a way that I wouldn't normally address her,

"Water! Fan!" I ordered, like some kind of slave owner.

And why did I need a fan? It was the middle of November. In London. And I permanently feel the cold. I definitely was not in my right mind here.

As for Ben, my wonderful, beloved husband and father to Léna and this soon-to-be-born baby, he was in the front seat with my dad, cracking jokes. The only way the two most important men in my life know how to deal with stress or difficult situations. And I suppose childbirth and labour fit into that category.

This pregnancy had been so different to my French one with Léna; this time around I was in London, my parents were just an hour's drive away, everything was in my mother tongue, but I had a child I needed to be thinking about. I was also older - a geriatric mum (who comes up with these terms? Apparently at 36 years old this is what you are) - and I could feel those 6 years in every stage of the pregnancy, and later on during the newborn months too.

Getting pregnant this time around hadn't been much easier than with Léna, the upside was that there was no miscarriage, which made for a less stressful pregnancy as I knew I'd already carried a baby to term successfully before.

Léna had been begging us for a baby sister pretty much from the day she was able to form the words, and after she broke her arm when she was 4 it was something Ben and I started discussing seriously. About 2 months after her accident I came off the pill and we started trying.

I was hopeful that it would happen quickly but yet again Mother Nature was determined to have me really want this baby. Despite trying for 8 months with Léna and 7 months with Clémence it looks like my body has a 'favourite period' to get pregnant as there are less than 4 weeks between their birthdays.

I did a very early pregnancy test with Clémence as we were due to help Tim move house; I had no problems carrying boxes up and down stairs, in and out of vans, as long as I wasn't pregnant. If I was pregnant I wanted to be as careful as possible. So the morning of

Tim's move I did an early morning pregnancy test (when it is most likely to pick up if you're pregnant or not) and had a faint positive line. Finally, the wait was over! Léna was still asleep and we weren't expected at Tim's just yet, so we had celebratory sex (celebratory sex as against the making-babies sex we'd been having for 7 months, in case you're wondering, it's so much better!).

I showed Ben the positive test, but as the line was faint he was doubtful (not having the encyclopaedic knowledge that I have on pregnancy tests after 15 months of trying). I tried to convince him it was real, and said I would tell my mum, dad and brother that day when we were all together.

Once at Tim's new flat he cracked open a bottle of bubbly and served all the adults a plastic cup of it. I knew I had to say something as otherwise my family would guess if they saw me not drinking, but I wasn't sure how to put it. So I announced to the room at large,

"it appears that I might be pregnant", to which someone quickly quipped,

"Why? Because you had sex this morning?"

I won't say *who* said it, but let's just they surprised themselves as it's not the type of thing they would normally say at all. And of all the days to say it, when Ben and I HAD just had sex that morning too, I quickly turned to Ben and in French reassured him that I hadn't filled my family in on the details of our sex life, and that this person was just making a joke!

Finally the message that I was pregnant got across and we told Léna that she was going to get a baby brother or sister, to which she replied in her 5 year old wisdom,

"if it's a brother I'm throwing him in the bin!".

Luckily over the course of the pregnancy we managed to get her to change her thinking, although she did still have a very strong preference for a sister, which made me a bit sad as I was convinced I was carrying a boy this time. Every single thing about the pregnancy felt different, the way I carried the baby, my cravings, everything. I was certain it would be a boy.

When I was 34 weeks pregnant I woke up in the middle of the night feeling distinctly off colour, I rushed to the toilet and felt like I'd had 10 curries the way things were rushing out of me. After a while I grabbed a sick bowl, as it looked like that end might see some action too, and clambered back to bed when the nausea eased off.

The next 24 hours saw me fighting with a nasty gastric bug which finally left me exhausted and more than a little worried about the health of my baby. My doctor sister, Kate, who lives in New Zealand and who had just had her second baby, reassured me via WhatsApp messages in the middle of the night that everything was probably fine as I was nearly full term.

As I could feel the baby kicking and I went back to normal fairly quickly I didn't go to the doctor's or get this checked out any further, not that I think it would have made much difference to what happened next.

At 35 weeks I had a check-up and I was asked if I had any symptoms of anything weird or if anything else was going on physically, I said that the only thing I could think of was I had really itchy palms. Which elicited a panicked look from the midwife and a trip to get a blood test done. The results of which seemed to indicate that I had an uncommon pregnancy condition called *Obstetric Cholestasis* (OC) which affects the liver and makes you itchy. The midwife informed me that the biggest risk with OC is that your baby is stillborn if you go to term, so she told me they would keep a close eye on me and they would induce me at around 37 weeks if my bloods showed signs of OC to avoid this happening.

I took this nice relaxing news home with me on the tube, stunned and gutted that another pregnancy was going to end in medicalisation. As soon as I was home I shared this information with my (retired nurse, mum of 5, trained midwife) mum and my (doctor, mum of 2) sister to see what they thought, before I started to panic. Luckily they recalled my recent gastric bug and both agreed it was highly likely my liver was all over the shop with that, rather than me having OC.

For 2 weeks I had to go to the hospital every few days for a blood test to check my OC score as I used to call it, and it would seem my family medics would be proven right as my bloods gradually went back to the usual levels, and we were able to take OC and early induction off the table.

Whilst it was a huge relief I also felt a bit cheated, for 2 weeks I thought I was going to have an early labour and get to see my baby at 37 weeks, and now I was back on a usual 40-42 week pregnancy schedule. Pfffff!

From 38 weeks onwards my midwife told me I could start doing things to encourage the baby to make an appearance - curries, a small amount of alcohol, pineapple, sex. Finally I felt like I was being allowed some good stuff again. Nothing happened though and the day before my (hospital) due date (40 weeks in the UK) I had a check-up, everything was looking good and my midwife gave me a sweep to see if that would get anything moving. (The hospital gave me my due date but I believe it was actually 3 days later and I'm the one who knew when the sex took place!!).

Two days after the sweep nothing much was happening and Ben really wanted to go and see the latest James Bond film with Tim; Madagascar 3 happened to be on at the same time and at the same cinema, so Ben and Tim went off to one screen while Léna and I went to the toilet before going to see the kids' film. Just as I was walking to the toilet I felt a very strange sensation going on in my knickers (nothing to do with the prospect of seeing Madagascar 3!), in the cubicle I discovered that - as I had thought - I had lost my mucus plug (if you don't know what that is Google it!).

Part of me was all "WOOHOO! It's happening!" and the other part of me was all "it had better not bloody happen now, we've just paid a fortune for our cinema tickets and those boys will not be happy if I pull them out of a James Bond film!".

We all made it through our films and back home with no sign of labour. I started to feel a bit gutted that this might be another Braxton Hicks-esque trick and that nothing was happening. Again.

Just to be on the safe side I had a curry, glass of red wine and pineapple for dinner, no harm trying and all that. But I regretted the curry after dinner when it decided to exit in a quick and liquid manner via the toilet.

It being a Sunday night I prepared Léna's school bag and uniform and, after a few more toilet trips, made it to bed and fell fast asleep. At around 2.30am I was woken up quite suddenly by a contraction. "Braxton Hicks, you won't fool me again!" I thought to myself, having called my parents up one evening, thinking everything was starting, only for it to calm down once they arrived after an hour's drive into London.

These contractions felt harder, stronger though, and like they meant business. However they were all over the place. 10 minutes apart, 7 minutes apart, 12 minutes apart. There was definitely no rhyme or reason to them. So I did what every good expectant mum does and picked up my phone; my app of choice back in 2012 was Twitter and I had lots of pregnant / new mum Twitter friends all over the world who I knew would answer my tweet about irregular contractions.

Despite every midwife telling me "it's not established labour until your contractions are regular" that didn't feel right. And Twitter agreed with me as mums flooded my feed with their irregular contractions which led to labour.

After spending 3 hours on Twitter conversing with other sleep-deprived pregnant / new mum friends I decided to call my mum at 6am, at which point Ben was alerted to the fact that today might be the day, as he had been sleeping, totally oblivious, the whole time.

"Hi Mum! So I got woken up by strong contractions at about half past two, and they're still coming but they're totally irregular, do you think it's worth you coming over?"

"How strong are they?"

"Well I'm having to…….(me doing contraction breathing as another one hits).....control my breathing through them."

"We'll be there in a couple of hours!"

After explaining to Ben how my night had gone and that I thought things might be happening, but I still wasn't sure, he got ready for work and got Léna ready for school, as I was spending all my time on Twitter, tracking my contractions and concentrating on my breathing.

As I was having breakfast with Léna (crunchy peanut butter on toast) my parents arrived. My mum took one look at me in the kitchen, holding on to the table, swaying my hips from side to side and mooing, and sent me to have a warm bath, not to see if they were Braxton Hicks this time but to slow labour down.

Despite all this Léna was completely oblivious to what was going on and took it all in her stride as just another normal Monday morning.

Just as Ben was about to drop Léna at school (fortunately just at the end of our road) my contractions decided to become regular, at 2-3 minutes apart. At 9am on a Monday morning in London, with a good 20 minute drive to the hospital. Mum and I told Ben to drop Léna and come back quickly as we had to hurry to the hospital; it was later on that I found out he'd been chatting to my school mum friends about how we were off to the hospital, that I was in labour, as if we were just off for a picnic, no rush at all!

On my medical records they have my labour down as 59 minutes because Clémence made her appearance into the world 59 minutes after I was checked in, something which no one in the hospital expected.

Despite my contractions being just 1-2 minutes apart at this stage, and incredibly strong, when I was examined I was only 4cm dilated. The midwife who was doing triage told us that she thought I would probably give birth around 2pm. But it was only 10am at this stage. I remember grabbing my mum's arm and, with what I'm sure was a crazed look on my face, telling her, "screw the midwife-led unit in that case, I'm going to need an epidural, I can't go through 4 more hours like this!".

Mum knew exactly what was going on though and in a soothing voice reassured me.

"let's just see how we get on, shall we?".

Although I was only 4cm dilated I was taken to a delivery room as my contractions were so close together and so strong. The midwife in there had obviously been told she had a while as I was only 4cm gone, as she was still getting the room ready and filling in paperwork when I felt ready to push.

I felt ridiculous saying I felt ready to push. I could see the clock on the wall, it said 10.30am. I knew that half an hour before I had been just 4cm dilated, and that you don't push at 4cm. So I didn't say anything first of all, but then it became too much and I blurted out,

"I need to push!".

The midwife looked a bit startled, this was all a bit fast after all, and asked me if my waters had broken yet; as they hadn't she told me I could push once to see if that broke them. Sure enough, Niagara Falls happened all around my feet and the floor - I hadn't even made it up onto the bed. The midwife proceeded to tell me that I could give birth as I was, standing up and holding onto the end of the bed. This suited me fine until she said to Ben

"and you will need to catch the baby as it comes out".

I looked down at the tiled floor at my feet and knew that I couldn't let that happen. I love Ben to death but he's not *Mr Sportsman of the Year*, what happened if he didn't catch the slithering bundle?!? As I was thinking this the midwife changed her mind and told me she needed me up on the bed so she could examine me.

As Clémence was doing her best to leave me via my back and all the pain was concentrated there I asked if I could stay on my front, which saw me in the one position I had previously decided I didn't want to give birth in. I was up on my knees, facing the wall with my lardy arse and cellulite thighs on display for the midwife, Ben and my mum to be treated to. I remember seeing this position in a book whilst pregnant and thinking,

"what an unflattering position to give birth in, I won't do that!".

Yet here I was, being given the all clear, I was fully dilated, I could push, and suddenly I didn't care about what position I was in, I could finally let go and meet my baby. I was asked if I wanted gas and air, which I fancied trying, but I couldn't tell you what it's like as in the end I was breathing through my nose and using the mouthpiece to bite down onto. After five minutes of pushing this baby out of my rear (or so it felt) it was over and there was silence in the room. I was still facing the wall and hadn't seen my baby yet, so I asked,

"what is it?" to which Ben replied "it's a girl!".

"What?!? Are you sure?!?"

I was so certain it was a boy this time round, I didn't mind either way but I couldn't believe these two such different pregnancies could result in two girls.

"You had better not want a son because I am not doing that again!" I told Ben as my newest baby girl was brought to my breast.

I had been so nervous about haemorrhaging again after Léna's birth, and the hospital wanted to make sure that didn't happen, so I was hooked up to a drip and we were left alone for most of the day, in our bubble of love, as I was required to stay lying down.

I was 36 years old and a mum of two beautiful daughters. After being so uncertain of what I was doing with Léna, I remember feeling so much more sure of myself with Clémence. It was this feeling of "well we've kept one alive so far, I think we know what we're doing!".

I was worried that a 6 year age gap would be bad, that our kids wouldn't bond or be friends, nothing could have been further from the truth. Léna was (and still is) the most devoted big sister, and Clémence worshipped (and still worships) the ground that Léna walks on. The plan was never such a big gap but I couldn't have planned it better. The only sad bit was having to answer people's blatantly rude questions:

"Oh, was that planned?"

"Is it the same father?"

"Did you struggle second time round?"

"Did you have IVF?"

The answers are yes, yes, not really compared to lots of couples our age and no. Not that it's any of your business!

After having Léna in France I was kept in hospital for 5 days and told when I got home that I needed to rest. I was made to go to appointments to have my pelvic floor muscles strengthened, where a midwife put her fingers inside me, asked me to sneeze, cough, laugh and pretend my vagina was a lift going up one floor at a time, all whilst asking me about my Christmas (Léna was a December baby).

After having Clémence I stayed in hospital one night because of my previous haemorrhage, and was home less than 30 hours after giving birth, with a much-photocopied piece of paper about doing pelvic floor muscles. The next day I did the school run with Léna, bundling Clémence up into her pram. 4 days after I gave birth I walked

10 minutes to the station, took the tube two stops along to Clapham Common and met my cousin and friend to watch the final Twilight film at the cinema. I was a bit tired and had to sit down gently but other than that felt fine (I'd left Ben with some expressed milk at home, which he didn't need to use as Clémence slept through my 3 hour absence).

The two experiences were so very different and if I had to choose I would go for giving birth in the UK (I can choose what position to give birth in?!?), but having my postnatal hospital stay in France. There is nothing worse than having to ask someone to watch your baby in a ward of 4 mums before walking down the corridor with your GIANT maternity sanitary towel in your hand! I seriously missed my en-suite bathroom, quiet room and sole roommate from France.

The one where I gave up yet another good job to follow my dreams

It was 2pm on a Wednesday in March and I was sitting in a cool and funky digital marketing agency's office in central London. 4 month old Clémence was at home being looked after by my mum so that I could come to this job interview. It had been fun getting dressed up for the work world, putting on make-up and heels, getting on the tube and reading my book, undisturbed by anyone during my 25 minute journey. But sat in the waiting room of this trendy office I got my first twinge of 'something's not quite right'. It wasn't the milk that was beginning to fill up in my breasts, I knew I had a few hours before I would need to get rid of that if I wanted to avoid pain. I had been excited about the idea of heading back to work, I had started to look at nannies' CVs, so what was wrong?

And suddenly it hit me, smack in the face, as I waited for my name to be called. This was wrong, so wrong. This wasn't what I wanted at all. I wasn't some kind of big career woman. I wasn't determined to climb the career ladder. I enjoyed my marketing job pre-pregnancy but I wasn't desperate to be the best and give my life over to it. Equally I wasn't all about babies and kids, wanting to spend my days forming and moulding the next generation. But there was one thing I was very clear about, as I sat there, ready to sell myself for a job that would take me away from my breastfed baby for a good 11 hours a day at least 4 days a week, this was not what I wanted. (I had a job to go back to but this one was better paid, and if I was going to pay for childcare in London I would need the highest salary possible.)

The interviewer calling my name broke into my reverie, it was time for me to go and answer their questions even though I no longer knew what I was doing there. The whole time we went through the job interview charade (as that's really what they are, isn't it?) my mind was flooded with a million thoughts of "if you don't want THIS then what do you want?!". The problem was I didn't know. Yet.

I didn't get my Kindle out of my bag on the way home, there was no point as I had a lot of thinking to do while I was in neutral territory. I made mental lists as the Northern Line made its way through Kennington and on to Clapham. I DIDN'T want to be out working in an office, but I DID want to do something. I DIDN'T want to be dependent on Ben financially (and anyway if we wanted to carry on living in a rental house in London we needed more than just one salary coming in). But I DID want to spend time with my kids. So what *could* I do that would enable me to spend time with my kids AND bring in money?

It came to me in a flash. I would be a nanny. I would look after our two girls and take in a couple of other kids which is where the money would come in. At the time I didn't know this role was called 'childminder' and not 'nanny', I just knew it was the solution to everything.

I hadn't allowed memories of Léna's early months into my head as I didn't want the sadness to come back, but slowly I admitted to myself that going back to work, leaving a breastfeeding baby behind again, might just break me completely the second time around.

I spent a few days researching everything before I even put the idea to Ben; I made a list of the pros and cons of becoming a childminder, taking the job I'd interviewed for or going back to my old job. I looked at time, money, logistics and what my gut was saying.

Ben wasn't convinced at first, but the more we discussed it the more sense it made to both of us.

Initially me retraining as a childminder sounded like a crazy idea; before going on maternity leave I'd been working as an Account Director at a digital marketing agency in central London, I had responsibility, respect, people who reported to me. I met with clients, used my brain, did fun things. I had Friday lunches out at the pub with colleagues, with short Friday afternoons leading into post-work drinks. Why would I give all this up for zero respect, zero brain work and no future?

Because I knew that it was the right thing for me to do at this stage of my life. I knew that my mental health depended on it. I knew that the health of our family needed it. I knew, without a shadow of a doubt, that it was the only thing I could possibly do at that stage.

I mentioned it to friends and school mums and got some surprising responses, quite a few people were shocked that I would lower myself to "wiping snotty noses and pooey bums", but I knew that this was what I needed to do.

And at times it was hard, I wasn't viewed the same way by certain people. I went from being an equal to being the hired help and that hurt, but I found the most incredible families to work for, and their children became best buddies with our two girls, and I became incredibly close with the mums.

I remember one day having a flash of realisation that this had been the absolute right thing to do. It was just after Clémence's nap, she must have been about a year old and as I went to pick her up from her cot she grinned up at me, I blew a raspberry on her tummy as I changed her nappy and she giggled that infectious laughter that only babies can, and any doubt was erased in a second. It didn't matter what happened on my CV or in my career for the rest of my life, these moments with her, and Léna, were more than worth whatever ended up coming next.

Task - how to know whether to be a SAHM, WAHM or working mum

One of the biggest decisions you make when you have kids is what you're going to do work-wise once they arrive. And it will be one of the first questions that people will ask you too. I became a mum in December 2006 and since then I have taken on all of these roles - stay at home mum, work at home mum and working mum. I have also loved and hated all of them at different times. If you're struggling to figure out what is right for you this may help:

- You don't have to choose ONE forever. Try it out, see if it works for you. Know that nothing is set in stone.
- Know that none of them is right, and none of them is wrong. Whatever is right for YOU is right for everyone. A happy working mum who sees her kids for 1 hour a day is far better than a miserable stay at home mum who's with her kids for 12 hours a day.
- Know that NO ONE else gets a say in this. Your partner can share his input and obviously you need to bear in mind any financial obligations, but at the end of the day this is what you will be doing for the majority of your waking hours, so it is your call.
- Look at the decision-making task again as you play around with different options and choices.
- Think outside of the box. There are SO many options open to you today. When I was growing up (in the UK in the 70s / 80s) I

knew one mum who worked. It just wasn't the done thing. There were very few options. Now there are more and more companies accepting flexible working, with fewer / different hours and days worked from home. You can easily set up your own business and work from home. And you can also stay at home with your kids, knowing that the job market is not closed to you afterwards.

- Don't let anyone make you feel bad or guilty about your choice. It really is nothing to do with them.

In Life Reboot Camp we look into this in more detail, with at least 3 women who've gone through the course changing their roles and ending up far happier. So don't be afraid to make that change, wouldn't it be great to be happier every day?

The one where Shouty Mummy reared her ugly head (again)

I was running late and I still wasn't ready to walk out the door. Everything had been going so well, I had planned, I had got up early. But you just can't plan for everything with kids and when you're solo parenting it's even harder. As I went to put Clémence into the double buggy I used for childminding she did the most explosive poo she has ever done. Scrap that, the most explosive poo any child has ever done. (If you're eating now you might want to put this book down until you're done.) I swear there was poo coming out the top of her vest and t-shirt, oozing out round her ears and right down into the feet of her tights.

It was one of those moments where you look up to the heavens and ask "WHY?!?" in a voice more than just a little tinged with hysteria.

I was working as a childminder which meant our changing table, wipes, nappies etc were all set up in our living room, but all Clémence's clean clothes were upstairs in her bedroom. So it took me a whole 10 minutes, even in my speediest nappy-cleaning, to get her cleaned up and ready to leave the house again.

At which stage I looked up and saw Léna dawdling through the kitchen, she hadn't brushed her teeth and looked in no way ready to leave the house. So I lost my shit. I couldn't expect the baby to know how much pressure I was under, but I thought Léna had understood just how much I needed her help while Ben was away for a week.

I had been trying to keep everything together, dealing with a nearly 7 year old, a nearly 1 year old, a dog that needed walking twice a day, but that I couldn't walk with the baby as he would pull the buggy over, and 3 cats.

As I let the words pour out of my mouth to chastise Léna for not being ready I wondered who I had become. I was sure I was the only mum in the entire world who felt the need to yell and scream at her kids. I was certain that I would never manage to have a happy, healthy relationship with Léna as I only seemed capable of yelling at her. I hated myself in that moment. I can remember it all so clearly. I wanted to crawl into a corner and cry. I wanted someone to come along and tell me they had it all under control, and I didn't need to worry about anything. Not kids, not groceries, not dinner, not laundry, nothing.

But there was no fairy godmother and Ben wasn't even on the same continent as me so I needed to go it alone. I finished my tirade and Léna started hers

"why don't you like me? I know you love Clémence more than me! I can't do anything right! I'm not coming with you!".

Instead of calming down and taking a deep breath, which is what I really needed to do to reassure and deal with my upset eldest daughter, I launched into another shouty mummy screaming session of

"I don't care whether you want to or not, you are coming with me!".

I was more than up against the clock. I had 5 minutes to do a 10 minute walk, except I had a recalcitrant nearly 7 year old, a half-filled double buggy and the pavements were filled with school kids and commuters. I made it to the front of Balham station just as the mum and little girl I childminded rounded the corner. I was a dripping mess, despite it being October in London, and Léna was doing her best teenage scowl, but I'd made it, somehow.

At least I hadn't dropped the ball on the work front, but I'd more than screwed up on the parenting front. Léna hadn't asked me to become a childminder, in fact she had loved having an au pair when I was a working mum, but now, instead of having a fun 19 year old German girl to hang out with her, she had a moody, overwhelmed, stressed out, tired mummy. Life really wasn't fair for her.

This was not how things were supposed to pan out. First of all in my dream showreel of parenting I was the perfect mum, I never shouted at my kids, we kissed, cuddled, laughed and giggled together. Also somehow in that video of "Sophie the perfect mummy" I enjoyed baking and crafting with them, who knows how that film reel got created as those are two things I abhor, with or without kids.

In my pre-parenting dream other mummies shouted at their kids as they weren't as good as me, because they didn't love their kids as much as I loved mine. I thought that it was all about them being bad mummies and not about the parenting gig being so bloody hard.

But it is, and it creeps up on you. You make it through the trench warfare of the newborn months, you start to get a handle on who this little person is and how they might slot into your family, then before you know it, out of seemingly nowhere you're losing your temper. That baby doll isn't as malleable as you'd first thought, and WTF! there is actually a person in there with a personality, likes, dislikes, opinions and everything.

I am not proud of the mum I've been at different times over the 12 years that I've been parenting. Don't get me wrong, I've been a bloody amazing parent at times, and as time goes by I certainly find being a mum easier, now that I've learnt how to make it work for me and my kids, but I've also been a really shit mum. I have no idea how many times I've roared (and I mean roared) at my kids, in particular Léna, who bore the brunt of most of my shitty parenting.

The good news is that I now know exactly why, when and how I turn from me, Sophie, Normal Mummy, into my evil twin, Shouty Mummy, who can't understand, empathise, listen or show any love to her kids. It is rare these days that I yell at my kids, and in fact Clémence probably wouldn't even associate shouting with me, but there used to be a time when the only character I played in our family movie was that of Shouty Mummy, and no one wanted to spend time with me, not my kids, not my husband, not even me.

Little by little I figured out what sent me over the edge. I analysed my behaviour, before, during (if possible) and after any outbursts. I looked at my kids' behaviour and I devoured information about parenting, behaviour, personal development, self-help and more, be it films, documentaries, podcasts, books or courses. I needed to learn and find a way to stop this monster in its tracks. And over time I have managed to pretty much tame the beast and become the mummy I always hoped and thought I would be. Well minus the crafting and baking in any case.

Task - how not to be Shouty Mummy

Shouty Mummy usually rears her head when there is something going on with YOU, so if you want to control this beast you need to check in with yourself. Ask yourself these questions:

- Have I had enough sleep / rest recently? Or am I feeling tired, drained and emotional?
- Where am I with my hormones (period, hormonal contraceptive, menopause or other)?
- When was the last time I took some time for ME? Time to recharge my batteries and put ME first?
- Am I spending too much time on a screen (phone, tablet, computer or TV)?

9 times out of 10 you will find that Shouty Mummy goes away once you pay attention to these 4 situations.

But sometimes Shouty Mummy comes out because of your kids. In which case ask yourself these questions:

- Have they had enough sleep?
- Have they had enough fresh air?
- Have they had enough physical activity?
- Have they had too much screen time?
- Have they had too much sugar? (Obvious sugar, like in sweets, but also hidden like in fruit drinks for example)

We can nearly always put Shouty Mummy to bed by dealing with these issues. It's not complicated but sometimes it can be hard.

If you found this task helpful you might want to download the free book bonuses which includes a PDF of all the tasks in this book, so you can go through them easily, whenever you need a reminder. Grab the bonuses here: www.SophieLeBrozec.com/happy-bonus

The one where I nearly got divorced

As I screamed "fuck you!" at Ben in front of our nearly 1 year old daughter one word kept rushing round in my head. *Divorce*. Even the sight of him made me see red and I couldn't imagine how our happily ever after could ever happen now. It had got so bad that I was wondering how things might pan out as and when we divorced. We lived in London where life is expensive, we had two kids and I was working as a childminder. How would we deal with things like finances, custody, living arrangements and all sorts.

That was back in 2013 with the same man who is my husband today, and who I'm madly in love with, but back then we'd let ourselves get to the edge of the precipice. We were stressed out, not communicating, sex was very much on the back burner and there was very little holding us together. I can talk about it now and see so clearly what was going on, but at the time I was in the middle of it, couldn't see my part in it all and was blind to anything except that he was an arsehole (in my 2013 opinion).

I was 37, we'd been married for 10 years but I didn't have a clue about how to deal with the hard times in a relationship, neither did Ben, so when things outside of our relationship put pressure on us we went from bad to worse.

When I was 27 I stood in front of that vicar, with a big grin on my face, and repeated after him "for better for worse, for richer for poorer, in sickness and in health" thinking that our love was invincible and that we'd never have to deal with any of that crap. How naive I was. How innocent and ignorant. But worse, why didn't anyone try and warn us?

Why didn't anyone tell us of the signs to watch out for? Why didn't anyone tell us how hard it is? Even when you marry your soulmate.

We nearly went over the edge of the cliff for fuck's sake! And we needn't have. If we'd had a clue about how to nip things in the bud, we could have saved such heartache, stress and sleeplessness. Thankfully we were given one book when we got married, it was from my parents' church in the UK as we had a wedding blessing there 3 weeks after our French wedding. As we couldn't attend the preparation for marriage lessons we were given a nondescript paperback book called "The 60 minute marriage" which made us laugh at the time "is that how long they think our marriage is going to last?!?" we both joked. My mum gave me the book and said she didn't know, all she knew was that she'd been asked to pass it on to us. It was one of the things that helped to save us.

There is so much I know now about relationships and marriage that I wish I had known back then, it was a harrowing time for both of us, and one we could have worked our way out of fairly quickly if we'd known what we were doing. As it was we were very lucky as we had a child-free week away in the Red Sea coming up, to celebrate our 10th wedding anniversary. I needed a holiday so much but, as I confided to an NCT (National Childbirth Trust) friend whose son was born a month after Clémence, Ben was the last person in the world I wanted to go on holiday with at the time.

I shared with her the struggles I'd had solo parenting while Ben had been away, and how he'd been driving me mad since he got back, and she gave me some incredible advice which I still remember, use and share with others. Her husband travelled a lot for business so she spent more time solo parenting her sons than she did sharing duties with her husband. She explained to me that every time her husband came back there was a bedding down phase, where everyone had to shift and settle back in to a new normal. She told me to hang on during that bedding down time and everything would probably be ok.

It was much harder than a bedding down phase that time around, but her words have helped me lots of times over the years. At the time I felt like I hated him and that I was pure white and he was the devil, I could not see beyond my own nose and I wondered what on earth would happen to us on our holiday.

My parents came over to stay with us and look after the girls while we were in Egypt for the week, and as we got ready to leave Léna started to play up. She was nearly 7 at the time and had never had issues with us going away on holiday without her before, but I think she'd clicked that she was going to be at school while we were on holiday, and wasn't best pleased! I had no idea what to say to her but I knew I needed that holiday more than I'd ever needed one in my whole life. I held her at arm's length, looked into her eye and said,

"Mummy needs to go away so she can stop being such a Shouty Mummy".

It sounded like I was checking into the Priory for a mental health problem, and to a certain extent I was. I felt out of control. I was a shit mum who did nothing but yell at her kids, my marriage felt like it was crashing down around my ears and I felt tired to my core. My words seemed to have the desired effect as Léna couldn't get me out of the door fast enough!

As Ben and I sat opposite each other in a generic diner at Gatwick airport, waiting for our flight to be called, we were miles apart. I don't recall a time I've ever felt so distant from my husband, the man

I had called my soulmate in our wedding ceremony just a decade earlier. What had happened to us? We weren't arguing, instead we were cold, each lost in our own thoughts about how much we needed this holiday.

I couldn't think about how to salvage our marriage at that stage, I needed to salvage me first. I was unrecognisable in the mirror and I had a real dislike for who I had become. One thing I did know was that I desperately needed time for me. It felt like when I gave up my full-time job to go on maternity leave, which then transformed into me becoming a childminder, I gave up all rights to have time off and time out. If I had a cold I had to keep going, night-time wake-ups, day-time kiddie duty. If I was tired I just had to go to bed as soon as the kids were in bed and hope no one woke me up during the night.

I had lost Sophie and who she was as a person, Sophie was now someone who worked out what to have for dinner, what groceries needed to be bought, when laundry needed to be done to ensure everyone had clean work and school clothes, someone whose waking thoughts revolved around breast feeds, nappy changes, lunch and dinner menus, school letters, outings to the park or to playgroup. Happy-go-lucky Sophie was gone, and I had the holiday to work out if she was dead and buried or just hidden down deep.

The first layer of tension eased away as I stepped from the plane into the warmth of Sharm-el-Sheikh in November. The second layer got shrugged off as I entered our hotel, took in the pool and the hotel room with no child's bed and no baby cot. The third layer fell off as I sat down to dinner with a glass of wine and concentrated on ME and what I wanted to eat. The next layer melted away in the warmth of the Egyptian sun as I lost myself in a book on my new Kindle by the pool.

Slowly the real Sophie was waking up and starting to claw her way back to the surface, at the same time as Ben's stresses fell away. Day after day our inability to communicate faded, we remembered who the other was, we talked about all the things that didn't matter, until we were ready to talk about those that did. The arguments and "fuck you"s were over by then, we were able to be gentle with each other, to hear why the other was hurting, to find solutions, to offer help to the other, and to put plans in place for life to be easier and more enjoyable for both of us upon our return to London.

By the end of our week in the Red Sea we were closer than we'd been on our honeymoon (and that's saying something), we were back in love again and ready to do what it took to make our marriage work and thrive. It scares me to think how close we came to losing everything and I work really hard now to not take my man for granted, and to make sure we have communication, love, respect and listening going on.

However I am far from perfect, as is Ben, and at times things slip, life happens, we get tired or stressed, we misinterpret words, looks, expressions and that cliff edge is never far away for any of us. But we both know what tools we can use now to keep us squarely on the path of a happy, thriving marriage, even if that can sometimes take time and / or money that we might struggle to find. We know that this is one thing we absolutely want and need to invest in, for us but also for our kids.

Task - how to avoid your marriage ending in divorce

This one task could be a book in itself so I'm going to try and give you an overview, because the work I've done on relationships with the women in my Life Reboot Camp is the work I'm the most proud of.

One woman, Michelle*, joined LRC telling me "it's my wedding anniversary today, and either this programme is going to help me get my marriage back on track or help me to go through a divorce". 6 months later Michelle and her husband had a fabulous Christmas together, with Michelle messaging me to say "I've got my husband back!".

Another Life Reboot Camper, Sarah*, told me that her relationship was robotic, transactional, it was all about teamwork as they dealt with their young kids and wasn't about the two of them anymore. After a few months of LRC Sarah happily messaged me to say that her husband was wondering what had happened to his wife, but that he was delighted, and she shared that their relationship was now going amazingly well.

Here are some of the things that Michelle and Sarah put into practice after doing the relationships module of Life Reboot Camp:

- Getting strict on 1-2-1 time - date nights, weekends away and so on (date nights can happen at home, so no complaints about money being an issue!)
- Accepting your share of the blame - that's right, you are not whiter than white!
- Working on communication - listening as well as speaking, careful choice of language and trying written communication if talking ends in arguments
- Balance at home - if one of you feels like you are doing more than your fair share of the work there will be resentment, so you need to work out a happy balance
- Sex - if this isn't happening enough you are in a friendship, not a relationship and that is often the kiss of death (after the work we did on this lesson Sarah told me that by mid-February her husband and her had had more sex than in the whole of the previous year!)

Obviously this is a whistle-stop tour of what you can do to work on your relationship, but hopefully it's a good starting point for you. If you do want to go deeper on this then consider joining Life Reboot Camp, we go into this in a whole load of detail, including a ton of tips on how to improve your sex life which was created based on an anonymous survey of everyone's biggest issues in this area.

* names have been changed

The one where we moved to a tropical island we'd never been to

30th October 2015 at Heathrow Airport. Crap! We're actually doing this. Our luggage has all been checked in, somehow we managed to stay within our 23kg per suitcase and 5kg per hand luggage each. Quite impressive for a nearly 40-something couple and their two kids. I had a ton more crap than that when I left home for university as an 18 year old.

I'm not letting on but I'm having waves of panic. What the fuck are we doing? We've never even been to Mauritius, and yet we're moving there with our two young kids. What if we hate it? What if the people are horrible? What if it stinks? What if there are tons of flies or other bugs or vermin? What if I can't handle being so far away from Mum and Dad?

It's just as well they're coming with us for the first month to help out with the kids, or I would officially be a mess of ugly tears right now.

A few months previously Ben and I made the big decision to leave London and move to Mauritius. A tropical island in the middle of the Indian Ocean, a 12 hour flight from the UK / France and from our families and friends. Also an island that we had never visited and where we knew no one.

We had originally moved to London to find work, but by early 2015 all Ben's income came via the internet and he could do that from anywhere in the world with a decent internet access. I was working as a childminder and a blogger, but I was in the process of creating online foreign language courses which I could do from anywhere.

London is very expensive, especially if you are renting, like we were. So Ben and I started looking at alternative locations as there was no point in throwing money down the drain when we could live in far cheaper places. We initially looked at South Wales as it wasn't too far from my parents. But within no time at all that idea went out the window when Ben suggested Mauritius.

"Hell yeah!" I replied, "errr, where is it again?"

I knew it was a tropical island. I knew it was a honeymoon destination and I knew that it had something to do with the French.

It turned out that it was in the Indian Ocean (in Africa to be precise, to the east of Madagascar), and not in the Caribbean as I'd initially thought. Also it wasn't a French island, in fact it hadn't been French since 1810 when it became part of the British empire. Just goes to show that I didn't have a clue. But as I looked out of the window at the grey, rainy London sky I didn't really care, a tropical island sounded so good.

We researched it A LOT more and discovered it ticked so many of our boxes. Hot, sunny, but not too hot, and no crazy weather extremes. Political stability. No terrorism to speak of. No dangerous bugs or animals. Advanced technologically, with high speed internet (vital for our work). Good schools and hospitals.

What more could we ask for? So we went for it. Selling or donating 90% of our belongings and heading off on the adventure of a lifetime.

I grin at my family sitting round me at the table in a forgettable restaurant in Heathrow airport. Tim has come along to say goodbye, which is nice but also makes it harder. Ben is trying to take a group photo of us all using his new selfie stick, and Dad and Tim are hiding their faces away at the shame of the selfie stick.

I love my family, why am I about to move half a world away from them? I smile at them all and pretend everything is ok. That everything is totally under control.

I know that my comfort zone is something that keeps me trapped if I let it. I know that all the fab, fun stuff lives on the other side of fear. I've discovered it for myself time and time again. But am I pushing things just a bit too far this time?

It's time to say goodbye, I force myself not to cry. I don't know when we'll be back. We literally have no idea what is waiting for us. Part of me wants to say "hold on! Change of plan! Let's just move back in with Mum and Dad," which is where we had been staying after giving up our rental house in London.

But I know I don't want to live a comfortable life, I want to live a fabulous life. I want to know that no matter what day I die I can say I lived my life to the max. I want to know that I did push myself, that I had dreams and I went for them, rather than steering clear and sticking with what is safe and known.

We are shown to our seats on the plane. Luckily there is a row of 4 seats so Ben, the girls and I can all sit together for the 12 hour night flight. I've been prepping nearly 3 year old Clémence in the run-up to the flight:

"Clémence, what are we going to do on the flight?"

"We're going to watch TV, eat and sleep!" She would parrot to me. (Well, something like that. As a bilingual child it sounded more like "*on va watcher télé, manger and dodo!*")

I had done everything possible to make the flight go as smoothly as possible. The girls and I had gradually been getting onto Mauritian time in the few days before our flight, which meant getting them up at 4am and putting them to bed at 6pm. They knew we would be sleeping for most of the flight. I felt very smug at how smoothly it was going to go.

But then mine and Ben's TV screens didn't work. We had these great black metallic boxes at our feet, under the seat in front, meaning even my little legs felt like they had no space. And then everything I'd briefed the girls on went out of the window as they realised they had unlimited TV, just for them.

I finally managed to get Clémence to sleep about 2 hours before we landed. As for nearly 9 year old Léna it was about 1 hour before we touched down. So you can imagine how fresh Ben and I were feeling as we landed in 28°C Mauritius!

We hit our first obstacle coming through immigration. Again I was feeling smug at how prepared I was, I knew all the papers I needed and I had them on my phone….oh crap! I had no internet connection and I'd forgotten to print out our return flight ticket, which we needed to prove we weren't staying in the country. Something we wouldn't need once Ben had applied for (and fingers crossed received) his Occupation Permit to live and work in Mauritius, along with his wife and two daughters.

This meant we only got a 2 month visa to stay, instead of a 3 month one. Making timings very tight for applying for the final paperwork, especially with Christmas and New Year thrown in to the mix too.

The next issue was we had given our UK mobile phone numbers to the taxi driver, but for some reason they weren't working in Mauritius at all. Fortunately the airport in Mauritius is not big at all, and we were the last ones to come through (thanks to immigration delays and the time it takes to gather suitcases for 4 adults and 2 kids, and go to the toilet!).

Finally we stepped out into the outside world of Mauritius and I KNEW this was the right decision. That sunshine. That blue sky. The warmth that penetrated right through to my constantly cold bones. We were in an airport car park but it seemed beautiful to me.

Our next plan seemed crazy to most people but for some reason it didn't worry us at all. We had signed a year-long lease on a rental house we'd found on the internet. In a country we'd never visited. Where we knew no one. And we were going straight there from the airport, meeting the estate agent at the house. Oh and whilst we were there a hire car guy was going to drop two cars off for us too.

Everyone seemed to think we were mad, but for us it seemed logical and normal.

After about an hour of driving we pulled up outside this giant house that was surrounded by all sorts of palm trees and coconut trees. As we walked through the garden, paying attention not to fall in the pool, Ben pointed out a banana tree too. It was very much a "pinch me" kind of moment.

The house was on 5 floors, had an independent apartment on the bottom floor where my parents would be staying, and you could see the sea from the top floor. It was 3 times the size of our narrow Victorian terraced house in London and cost us a third in rent.

Despite no one having slept for more than a few hours on the plane we were all buzzing as we explored the house. Until the girls started complaining that they were hungry. By this time it was 3pm local time (11am UK time) and we'd not eaten since breakfast on the plane quite a few hours before.

But we couldn't go and do any shopping until the landlord had arrived, so we were waiting when the doorbell rang. We didn't bother even looking up - we knew no one in Mauritius so it wasn't going to be for us. Except it was!

In the run-up to leaving the UK I had got in touch with a few people in Mauritius who I'd found online through forums and Facebook. One of whom was Priscille who (amongst other things) runs a Facebook page called *Discover Mauritius Island*. I'd been in touch, asking her questions before we arrived, and she was incredible about getting back to me. We clicked as we chatted online and became Facebook friends.

When we arrived at our new home I had quickly shared a snap from Léna's bedroom window on Facebook to let everyone know we'd arrived safely and that it was glorious. Priscille had seen this photo, and knew exactly what house we were renting. She had gone out to the local supermarket and bought us a welcome basket of snacks including bread, French saucisson, cheese, chocolate and more.

If I hadn't known we'd made the right decision before that moment then Priscille and her husband Fred's arrival and welcome basket sealed it.

We had arrived. I was living in a dream house. On a dream island. Living 17 year old Sophie's dream of a French-speaking tropical island. I was 3 months away from my 40th birthday and felt happier than I had done in years. Everything was going to work out just fine.

The one where I broke myself and missed Léna's birthday

The red digits on my alarm clock flashed 2.47am but I couldn't really take it in as I lay in a strange position on my right hand side, cradling my left arm in the opposite hand. As I tried not to change position I let out an almost silent wail, then sucked my breath in through my teeth. The pain was excruciating; I can honestly say that childbirth was a walk in the park in comparison. I couldn't move, yet staying in that position barely took the edge off the agony. Ben couldn't understand what was going on and wanted to know if he should drive me to the hospital. But I knew there was nothing to be done just yet, I was booked in for an MRI scan to find out what was going on inside my arm, shoulder and neck, until then I was fully dosed up on meds and the only thing to do was sit and wait.

I don't believe in regrets; I am decisive and I live a life with a certain amount of risk and know that bad things can and do happen, but I don't let that stop me from living. However I think I can safely say that I had one big, fat regret in my life: not going to the doctor's sooner when my arm / shoulder / neck started hurting.

It was a stupid thing, a bit of a dull ache in my upper left arm. I'd noticed it when we were travelling in Europe June - August of 2017 and I put it down to sleeping in weird places combined with packing, unpacking and lugging suitcases around. I assumed it would just go away eventually.

We got back to Mauritius and it still hadn't calmed down a few weeks later. I had to go and see the doctor with Léna one day so I mentioned it when I was there, and he prescribed me an MRI and sessions with an osteopath. With travel and waiting time it would take me half a day to get the MRI done, and each osteopath session meant at least an hour and a half out of my day. So I added both to my to do list, aiming to get to them when I had time.

Days passed, then weeks and they were still on my list, still not done. I was sometimes woken up at night by my arm, but it wasn't serious (yet) so I kept ignoring it and telling myself I would get round to sorting it out. Until the decision was taken out of my hands.

It was about 10 days before Léna's 11th birthday and the pain suddenly got worse, I found myself in tears one afternoon as I popped painkillers and finally made an appointment for an MRI, but they couldn't squeeze me in for another week. And I couldn't see the osteopath until I had the MRI results. So I told myself I'd just have to suck it up. Until the day before Léna's birthday when the pain was almost unbearable, so I made an emergency appointment to see an osteopath, despite neither of us really knowing what he was dealing with, but I needed to do something.

As I climbed into the car I thanked my lucky stars that we chose to get an automatic car as my left arm was almost completely immobilised (steering wheels are on the right in Mauritius, like in the UK) and there was no way I could have changed gears. As it was I had to use my right hand to reach across and move from park into reverse or drive, my left was held gingerly at my side.

The visit to the osteopath helped a tiny bit but he didn't want to do much until he knew exactly what was going on, after the MRI. So I took my still very painful arm and shoulder home and told myself I would be well enough to go swimming with dolphins in the wild the next morning for Léna's birthday.

But that evening it became clear that there was no hope in hell of that happening, I could barely move in bed let alone haul myself onto a boat. I was devastated. Why had I been so fucking stupid? I'd thrown on this martyr coat and had been wearing it for months, because I 'didn't have time' to look after my own health. I had no issue taking my kids to doctor's appointments but for some reason I had decided that my health didn't warrant the same level of importance, and I'd pushed it so far down my to do list until my body literally rebelled.

I was so angry with myself. I missed out on an incredible experience with my daughter because I hadn't listened to myself, I had convinced myself that mums sacrifice themselves for their kids, that they don't deserve to put themselves first. And everyone suffered because I couldn't look after myself. Ben had to help me get dressed - have you ever tried to put a bra on with a mashed up arm?! Léna had to help me deal with food if Ben wasn't around. Clémence had to sort herself out too despite only being 5. And my business had to be put on the back burner for a while as I couldn't type or sit properly.

My regret is that I didn't get that MRI done straight away, that I didn't start off those osteopath sessions straight away, that I waited until I had no choice before actually looking after myself. And it wasn't just me who suffered, but the whole family, as I tried to prove some stupid point that I was invincible.

Needless to say it hasn't happened since and I now put myself on the top of my list, because if I go down I take everyone down too.

Task - how not to burn out

Us women, especially us mums, don't know how to say "no" so we keep going, and keep going, and keep taking more on, until our body slams on the brakes and we crash and burn. Either our mental health suffers, or our physical health, or both. But we feel like people will judge us if we don't do ALL the things, and do them perfectly.

The thing is when we burn out we take everyone down with us. Because if we can't do the school run, and make packed lunches, and check school bags, and buy groceries, and cook dinner and so on it means someone else has to pick up those pieces.

Guilt stops us from putting ourselves first. We feel selfish if we *dare* to think of ourselves before others, but it's even more selfish to push all your chores and household tasks onto your partner / children's shoulders because you DIDN'T put yourself first.

Now you know that you need to avoid burnout, how do you go about doing that?

- Listen to your body. Are you tired? Do you need more sleep? Are you feeling overwhelmed? Do you feel mentally drained? Listen and obey. Go to bed early, say no, switch off devices and your brain.

- Keep an eye on your calendar - colour code it if you can so you can make sure it's balanced out with family stuff, work stuff and downtime for you. Adjust if need be.
- Go to the doctor when it's a niggle, not when you're in full-blown agony. Believe me on this one!
- Make sure you are putting yourself first. This is the best way to avoid burnout. Put your priorities at the top of the list, this is a surefire way to be a better wife and mum anyway.
- Don't bite off more than you can chew - every time you say yes to something / someone it means saying no to something / someone else. Make sure your yeses to others do not mean nos to your health and wellbeing.

Don't forget to download the free book bonuses, especially the checklist on how to be happy and the motivational audio, these will both help if you struggle with burnout. You can grab all the bonuses here: www.SophieLeBrozec.com/happy-bonus

The one where I didn't know what business to run

I'd been running online programmes teaching English to French-speakers and French to English-speakers, but it no longer made my heart sing. I wanted to make a difference. I wanted to do something big. But I didn't know what. In March 2017 I retired my mummy blog (FranglaiseMummy.com) and launched www.SophieLeBrozec.com with a tagline of "Love the life you live!" but that was all I had. I knew I wanted this to be my business. But doing what?

While I waited I blogged. And shared stuff on social media. And built up my mailing list. But I had NO idea what product or service I was going to actually sell. Ben was keen for me to get something out there - understandably - but I was creatively empty. I finally picked a topic that I enjoy and know lots about, and set about creating an online course on it.

The topic was decision-making. I had a free video guide on the subject that was popular, so I thought I'd create a programme about how to make decisions. My heart wasn't in it but I knew I had to do something. I struggled to come up with a name for the course and called it - the very un-catchy - "*What should I do?*".

I re-read *Launch* by Jeff Walker and set about creating sales videos. I scripted them and filmed myself as I read from the teleprompter. It felt so icky and wrong, but I did it as everybody else was doing this and telling me it was the way to launch an online course.

Then two things happened. First, Léna got sick. It turned out to be nothing major (thankfully) but for a while we thought it might be something very serious. So I was beside myself with stress and not sleeping. At the same time I booked in some one-to-one sessions with Marie Houlden to do some energy work as I felt so *wrong* and I couldn't figure out why or what was going on. It was the first time I'd done any work of this kind and I didn't really know what to expect. After the first session I felt relaxed, calmer, but not like I had any answers. Then in between my first and second sessions I had a revelation.

I remember it so clearly. It was a Tuesday evening and I was standing in the kitchen, heating up leftovers for dinner, when I had a light bulb moment. I realised I was trying to be someone I wasn't and do something I didn't feel good about. No wonder everything felt out of whack. I made the instant decision to shelve the course, for the time being at least. Ben couldn't understand why I was doing it. I had a course idea. I had a mailing list with people interested. I had sales videos that had been recorded and were ready to go. I had a half-created course. Why would I dump it? But I knew I wouldn't make many sales as it just felt wrong, and I knew I wouldn't show up as my best self for those clients for the same reason.

Despite having already announced that the course was coming, on social media and to my mailing list, I pulled it all. I just *knew* it was wrong. Over the next two sessions I had with Marie I felt such relief at having made this decision. And I knew it was the right one without a shadow of a doubt. But I was still stuck as I still didn't know WHAT product or service to offer in my business.

I gave myself permission to take a break from stressing it all. It was November 2017 and I'd spent 8 weeks travelling in the UK, France and Ireland in the previous June-August, just before that we'd had to pack up our old house and find a new house, with us moving into our new house straight from the airport after our trip. This then led straight into Léna being ill, my parents came to stay with us for the whole of November (which I LOVED but which is not conducive to getting work done), then from mid-December until late January we had Ben's family staying with us. So I gave myself permission to switch my brain off from trying to find a solution, and over Christmas I took a break from everything online. I chilled out. I went walking in nature.

Suddenly, one random day in December, when I was least expecting it, I *knew* exactly what I was meant to do. Everything. In a flash I had a name, a module structure, individual lesson ideas. Everything. It would be an online course for women, called *Life Reboot Camp*. It would be comprised of 6 modules covering every area of their personal and professional life.

I barely had time to scribble down the modules as my brain was going so fast. It reminded me of a quote by Marianne Williamson:

"Remember God is the water, you are the faucet."

(I'm an atheist so I substitute 'the universe' for 'God' and I'm a Brit so 'faucet' becomes 'tap', but the message is the same!)

This was exactly how it felt for me. It didn't feel like I was coming up with these ideas, they were flowing through me, from my brain to my fingers, from my fingers to the keyboard. I just needed a clear head and mind for everything to take form.

In the space of just a few hours I'd gone from not having a clue to having a super clear offering, with a name, a structure, a price, a sales page, everything. However I knew I would not be doing a 'launch' like the one I'd attempted before. It still felt so wrong and icky. I went against all suggestions and recommendations that this was the ONLY way to go and I just launched my way.

I can't begin to tell you the buzz I got as my first sales came in back in February 2018. Finally I had found my purpose. This was what I was supposed to do.

As I celebrated 1 year of Life Reboot Camp in February 2019 I did a tally. There were nearly 80 Life Reboot Campers from 4 continents, 8 countries and 7 nationalities. I had already helped save 2 marriages, helped one person happily end an unhappy marriage. I had helped several women figure out what they wanted to be doing work-wise, had reduced Shouty Mummy levels in numerous households and was partly responsible for tens of happier women all over the world.

Yep, this was what I was supposed to hold out for.

(If you are interested in joining Life Reboot Camp please DON'T sign up via the sales page on my website, instead go to www.SophieLeBrozec.com/camp-book where you get a reduced rate as a reader of this book.)

The one with my everyday life in Mauritius

The sea all around me was like a mirrored lake, with barely a sound to be heard, the sun had not yet risen behind the funny-shaped mountain and the light was a strange grey, tinged with pale pink. I looked out at the water around me and marvelled at how the sea, in the middle of the Indian Ocean, with very little land all around, could be so calm, so still. My thoughts were quickly interrupted as our skipper called out to us "there they are!" my eyes followed his finger and I watched a pod of dolphins swim past our boat. Everyone on the boat got busy, grabbing fins, putting on masks and snorkels, and I joined in. Within 1 minute of spotting these beautiful creatures I was swimming alongside them, listening to their funny squeaking noises in the water, and trying to keep my mouth shut around my snorkel, when it wanted to be wide open in wonder. Some of them were close enough for me to touch had I stretched out my hand (I didn't), and I felt such a sense of peace and of something so much bigger than me as I swam in their world with them.

As they swam away from me I lifted my head up and watched as my two young daughters swam alongside the dolphins in the water too and I silently thanked myself. For making that decision. For being brave enough. For leaving my comfort zone. This was worth any pain, stress and questions from others about the sanity of our choice. We hadn't known what Mauritius would bring, we literally didn't know a thing when we decided to move here. Would we fit in? Would we like it? Would we make friends? Would the girls settle in? Would we even get the paperwork necessary to live on the island? We didn't know.

We had more unanswered questions than answers, but we went with our gut and what felt right.

And on that day, as I swam with dolphins in the Indian Ocean, as the sun rose from behind the mountain, and as I watched my own little fishes swim alongside those elegant sea creatures, I knew without a shadow of a doubt that this was where we were meant to be. This was where our path was meant to lead us. This was our home, our life, our future.

But let's be honest, we don't go swimming with dolphins at sunrise every day, partly because even that spectacular event would get boring if you did it too often, and partly because we still have businesses to run, kids to get educated, food to get on the table and all the other usual everyday routines and chores of a family of four. So what does my everyday life in Mauritius look like?

As I sit and write this it is April 2019, we have just celebrated Easter and I am aiming to get this book written, edited and published by June when I'll be in the UK. At the same time I am launching a new course with the incredible Marie Houlden, called Self First. I have also just finished reading Chillpreneur by Denise Duffield-Thomas and Do Less by Kate Northrup, so I am embracing the idea of being productive yet not ignoring my own self-care, of putting my work out into the world to help women as best I can, yet not pushing myself to burnout in order to do it, so this is what my everyday life looks like:

I get up at 5am (about an hour before sunrise) and I do an hour of *Miracle Morning*. This idea is from a book of the same name by Hal Elrod, the aim being to get up an hour earlier than you have to in order to start your day the 'right' way, to be in the right mood, frame of mind and productivity. So from 5am to 6am I journal, I do EFT (Emotional

Freedom Techniques also known as tapping), I read motivational books and I prepare my day calmly and peacefully.

From 6am to 7am I wake 6 year old Clémence up, get her showered, dressed and ready for school with breakfast, packed lunch etc. She is pretty good at doing most of this herself, I just need to be behind her to keep her on track as the school bus collects her shortly after 7am.

At which time Léna starts getting up for her day, but at 12 years old she doesn't need much input from us, just some kicking up the backside as she's not a morning person, which means I can concentrate on myself again and I do some kind of a workout. That could be a 5km run in the forest near where we live, soaking up all the positive energy there, or the 30 day shred DVD, or I go and do a Pilates lesson on the beach.

Léna is now homeschooled, she has a study course to follow and rarely needs our help or input, so she is pretty much autonomous and Ben gets on with his work from home too. So every morning the three of us head to our respective rooms / offices to get on with our day's work. I don't generally have breakfast during the week, I do intermittent fasting where I don't eat between 7pm and 12.30pm the next day. I find it works great for my mental clarity, for my physical capabilities and it's a great way to help me keep my weight in check too!

Depending on what workout I've done I'm usually at my desk, ready to crack on by 8am or 9am tops. My phone is almost permanently switched to "do not disturb" mode which means those in my favourites can get through but pretty much no one else can, and I tend to place my phone out of reach so I'm not tempted to pick it up. I also have no notifications on my computer and even on Facebook I have Chrome newsfeed eradicator which means I can't see my newsfeed if I do need to pop on for any reason (such as to check in with my groups there).

Everything I do is set up so I'm as productive as possible and so I waste as little time as possible. By working this way I've managed to put numerous online courses out into the world, to write this book (and a bilingual children's book a few years back too), to market my various businesses but to also spend time on ME, with Ben and with our girls.

I am a real morning person and I get my best (and most of my) work done by lunchtime, I also LOVE the work I do and find that the morning speeds by without any breaks or stops until it's time to eat with Ben and Léna around 12.30pm. Ben and I split the household chores and he makes us lunch most days, so I literally stop for lunch and my meal is ready and waiting for me (which I love!).

At lunchtime we tend to eat a big salad or Buddha Bowl in front of the TV, mostly old episodes of Friends, Modern Family or something similar. We do this so we switch off from our work; often if we eat at the table we end up talking work or Léna's studies which helps none of us to switch off!

Sometimes after lunch I will lie in the garden reading my book, or I might meditate. In general I take about an hour off for lunch and I try to switch off as much as possible as I know I can then give my best in the afternoon. I have spent years not taking lunch breaks, because I didn't have enough time and there was always too much to do. But the thing is I'm never going to get to the bottom of this to do list, however I might hit Burnoutville and not be able to work or function anymore, so now I'm super strict around lunch breaks.

If there are no after-school activities then my afternoon can go on until anything between 5pm and 6pm, depending on what I want to get through and how much I'm listening to myself. Around 3pm I take a break when Clémence gets in from school, we have a cuddle and a quick chat about how her day was, then we sit down and do a bit of reading together, before I leave her to have a snack and play as I return to my desk.

At 6pm we all sit down to eat as a family, in general this happens at the dining table. We eat this early because we all want to eat together and because Clémence is a BIG sleeper so needs to be in bed by 7pm to be able to cope with waking up at 6am.

After dinner Clémence clears the table and Léna does the washing-up. Both girls have been doing chores since they were little as it's so important to us that they learn we are a team, and that we all have to pull our weight to make the team work. Once the clearing up has been done the girls go off to bed, around 7pm for Clémence and 8pm for Léna though she might read in bed. So from around 7pm Ben and I are pretty much done with our duties for the day so we either curl up on the sofa to watch a film or a series, or we read together side by side on the terrace by the pool.

Once a week we have a date night where we head out to the cinema or to a restaurant, or we have a nice meal at home, just the two of us once the girls are in bed / in their bedrooms. This is vital for our relationship as otherwise we find ourselves just working on the parenting team together and not actually connecting as a couple.

Because we get up so early we're usually in bed by 9-9.30pm at the latest. Our bedroom leads out to a terrace and before I go to bed I go and stand out there, look up at the stars (which you can see really well from where we live) and give thanks. Either in my head or out loud I give gratitude for my day, my life, my health, my family, my business, depending on how I'm feeling. It gives me such a great positive boost before I head to bed to lose myself in a book before falling asleep. So that's what a typical day in my dream life in Mauritius looks like.

The one with my happily ever after

I'm sure you want to know, am I living my happily ever after now?

The answer is yes and no. I am ridiculously happy and fulfilled. Mauritius, my marriage, my kids, my business are everything I had hoped they would be, and more. I am so incredibly grateful for everything that I have and for the journey that led me to be here, living this life. So yes, I am living my happily ever after. But at the same time no, I'm not.

There are times when I forget to practise what I preach. When I am a bitch to be around because I haven't taken enough time for me. When I roar at my kids. When I'm a shit to Ben. I've discovered that no amount of living in paradise, with swimming pools, cocktails and beach sunsets will fix you if you don't do the inner work. If you are not aware of who you are and how you are, and the control you have over your own life and your own happiness.

If I'm not careful I don't live my happily ever after, so I am on a lifelong journey of personal development, to be aware of what pushes my buttons and to do my best to avoid falling into the hellhole of Shouty Mummy and Nagging Wife syndrome.

And of course I still have goals that I want to achieve. I want quadruple figures of women in my Life Reboot Camp so I can really start making a difference. I want to do more speaking gigs, appear on more podcasts, and why not even do some TV work? I want to share this message far and wide so that more and more women can be happier. Which has a knock-on effect of their circle being happier, which ripples outwards. That is my goal. That is my purpose. That is MY happily ever after.

Task - how to get YOUR happily ever after

It's all well and good knowing what my happily ever after is, but how do you get YOUR happily ever after? First of all you need to be super clear on what exactly that looks like.

For years I wanted to go travelling with our family on a kind of a gap year. We planned it all out - 6 months in a camper-van travelling around Europe, and 6 months in a camper-van travelling around the US and Canada. We had a route mapped out, we knew what we were going to do with our home, our belongings, our pets, the kids' schooling, everything.

Then one day, very recently, I realised that this wasn't my happy ever after. That wasn't my goal. It was something I had picked up from others, liked the sound of when I was trying to escape from a life I didn't love, but it certainly wasn't what I wanted now. Luckily Ben wasn't as gung-ho about the gap year idea as I was and had no issue with canning the idea.

So be very careful that your happily ever after dream is YOUR dream and not somebody else's. Living on a tropical island is very much MY dream, but that doesn't mean it is right for YOU.

Get clear on what your dream is. What does your happily ever after look like? If you're not sure, start by journaling what you DON'T want as sometimes that is so much easier than working out what you DO want.

Where do you NOT want to be living? What do you NOT want to be doing? Once you're clear on that it's easier to figure out the opposite. You don't want to live on a tropical island? No problem, do you want to live in the mountains? In a big city? In the countryside?

As you list your happily ever after get really clear on what makes you happy. You can't just say "I want to be happy" or "I want to have lots of money" as these things are too vague. What does happiness look like for you? What does it mean to you to have lots of money? Drill down and get clear on what all this means for you.

Maybe happiness is time to yourself or dinner out with your other half. Maybe money is freedom to do what you want at the weekend.

What makes me happy in my life? It's the silly, little things like being around when 6 year old Clémence comes home from school, gives me a hug and tells me all about her day. Or when Léna confides in me as she knows I am not stressed, that I am present and I am listening. It is going to the beach with Ben and a couple of beers to watch the sun set, or lying side by side outside, looking up at the stars. It's getting dressed up in 1980s clothes and going out dancing with my girlfriends.

Whilst swimming with dolphins, boat trips and swimming pools in the garden are all wonderful, that is not what brings lasting happiness and fulfilment. In fact you'd be amazed at how quickly that becomes mundane and ordinary.

If I had to choose between the dolphins, the sunshine and my paradise lifestyle but with non-communicative kids and husband OR a tiny house in a shitty town in the UK, with grey weather but with loving and communicative relationships with Ben and our girls then that decision would be a no-brainer. (Just in case you're wondering it would be the tiny house in the shitty town in the UK!)

Get clear on what makes you happy and then work out how to get there. Look back over the task chapters in this book and see what you can do to improve the different areas of your life (or download them as a PDF file here: www.SophieLeBrozec.com/happy-bonus). Be aware of what makes you sad or angry and what makes you feel happy and alive. When was the last time you shouted? What brought it on? When was the last time you laughed? What brought it on?

You have 100% control over how you feel, don't give that power away to anyone else. As Dorothy discovers at the end of The Wizard of Oz, she had the power to go home by herself all along. And you have had the power to be happy by yourself all along.

Conclusion

Thank you for letting me take you on this journey lovely. I hope you have got tons of help, tips, ideas and tools from reading my book, and I hope you feel less alone too. Here are some things you can do moving forwards…

Download the free bonuses that accompany this book:

1. A PDF of all the task chapters in one easy-to-access document.
2. A simple checklist of how to be happy for you to print out and refer back to on tough days.
3. An audio version of the book (in case you prefer listening to reading).
4. A motivational "kick up the rear" audio from me, to listen to when you need a pick-me-up.

To access all these free book bonuses just head to www.SophieLeBrozec.com/happy-bonus

If you want to go one step further and really turn things around for yourself, do check out my **Life Reboot Camp**. All readers of *How to be happy…* can get lifetime access for a reduced rate. For more information just head to www.SophieLeBrozec.com/camp-book

Life Reboot Camp is made up of 6 modules that you do in your own time, with the support of our incredible community:

Module 1
All about YOU
Module 2
Woo-woo

Module 3
Relationships & Friendships
Module 4
Parenting
Module 5
Work & Career
Module 6
Decision-Making & Facing your Fears

Each module is made up of video / audio lessons and worksheets. I am busy and don't have time for anything more in my life, and I'm guessing you're the same, so I've made this as easy as possible to squeeze into your life. Each lesson is just 10-15 minutes long and you can either watch the video or listen to the audio. Lots of my Life Reboot Campers have found it easy to listen to the lessons whilst commuting, cooking the dinner or sitting around waiting for their kids to finish their after-school activities.

"When I signed up to Sophie's Life Reboot Camp, it was the first time I signed up to an online course. Would it be worth the money? And most of all, would I have time to actually do it? These were my 2 main fears but after a few months, I can honestly say that this was the best decision I've made! You get the course material for life so the investment is 100% worth it. And because it is full of easy-to-follow practical advice, I set time aside every day to listen to the modules as and when I needed to work on a particular area of my life. What I love is that the course covers all aspects of your personal and professional life. It has had a huge impact on my mindset, the way I deal with my business and my general happiness within my family. So yes, definitely, I would recommend Sophie's Life Reboot Camp if you would like to "find your better you"."

Violaine Kangou - Translator and mum of three

"I thought I didn't need Life Reboot Camp, I thought everything was ticking along quite nicely, but my children were going off to school, getting bigger, and I was thinking is this it? Then I got into Life Reboot Camp and discovered there was actually a whole load of stuff that needed doing. I highly recommend Life Reboot Camp, it's made such a difference to my life."

Sally Farrant - Financial Controller and mum of two

Now go and live that one beautiful, fabulous, sometimes shitty, life. It's short, it's fragile, it's precious. Look for the beauty and you will easily find it. Look for the shit and it will find you.

Acknowledgements

I've got about a zillion people to thank but I don't want the acknowledgements to be longer than the actual book, so I'm going to try and keep it concise! This book would never have seen the light of day had it not been for certain people and situations. I've had a vague idea of this book in my head for the last 20 years. Every time something shit happened and I came out of it, alive and stronger, on the other side I would tell myself "one day I'll write a book about all this". But that one day never came.

Then a few things happened. In 2018 I did Marie Yates' writing course which got me thinking seriously about book writing again, so thank you Marie. Then in February 2019 I was out doing my usual weekly walk and a solid idea for a book slid into my head. I got home and wrote it down. A couple of weeks later I stumbled across a post from Leonie Dawson about a new online course she was launching - 'Finish your book in 40 days' - and something inside me said "you have to get that!".

I sat down to write this book on Wednesday 3rd April 2019. I wrote for an hour every day. I just kept going. So thank you Leonie. For the course. For the accountability. For the constant "Write your fucking book!" messages. I finally did it. And here is my fucking book :-)

Thank you to Charlotte Broster of Charlotte Broster Photography for the fabulous cover photo and author pic, I love them both!

When I moved to Mauritius I knew no one here, and was worried about not having a support network. We had the best welcome EVER from Priscille and her husband Fred, and I can never thank them enough for their love, support and reassurance that we'd made the right decision. From the very first day we arrived, and for every day since. They are the loveliest people in the world, and if you are ever in Mauritius do check out Fred's business, Sea 2 Peak Adventures, which offers the most incredible mountain hikes.

Thank you to all the incredible women in Mauritius who helped me create my circle of friends here when it was time to start from scratch. There are too many of you to mention but a special shout-out to all the Tamarin ladies who joined the book / wine club I set up when I arrived. And a special thank you to Mandy for being my best friend, neighbour, partner in crime and someone to lean on when things get tough.

Before starting afresh in Mauritius I had to create a new group of friends and support network in London. Thank you Jo, for being a fabulous next door neighbour, thank you for your continued friendship, even after we left London, and especially thank you for letting us use your house as a hotel when we come back to London.

I was told, before I moved to London, that people in London are rude and unfriendly, that people don't care about or speak to their neighbours. I am so pleased that they were proven wrong. Thank you Beth, who got the ball rolling with the Scholars Road neighbourhood watch, which led to the first book / wine club, which led to girls' nights out, which led to the Scholars Road babysitting circle. A big thanks to all of you for bringing such joy and fun to my life when I was at a low point, especially Jo, Beth and Karen.

Thank you Tim and Becky for the mid-week casual nights in. Thank you for putting the girls to bed when I couldn't face them anymore. Thank you for all the fun and laughter. If there is one thing I miss the most from London it is these evenings.

Thank you to Sally and Katie for being the best mums a childminder could hope to work with. Thank you for your ongoing friendship and a special thank you to Katie for the constant support with my business and this book.

Thank you to all my Nice friends, the French ones and the expats, the ones who supported me through the hard times, and the ones who partied with me in the good times.

From my time in London onwards I have been on a continual discovery of incredible mentors who I have learnt so much from. Thank you to all the women who have gone before me and taught me so much - in no particular order, Denise Duffield-Thomas, Marie Forleo, Gabby Bernstein, Carrie Green, Gemma Went, Glennon Doyle, Brené Brown, Liz Gilbert, Oprah. And a special thanks to Marie Houlden who has helped me peel back layers and layers of the onion that is my mindset, inner dialogue and emotional blocks. I had no idea of the impact that Marie would have on me when I first started working with her in 2017, but it has been a real game-changer, so thank you Marie.

Now onto the thank yous where I know I will struggle to find the words.

Thank you to my parents. I know you don't 'get' what I do or why I need to air my dirty laundry in public, but thank you for accepting how important this is for me, and for letting me get on with it. Thank you for never pushing me to conform to what "Society" says I should do. Thank you for the constant support and love.

Thank you to Ben. I don't even know where to start. There is a whole book I could write on this subject. Thank you for putting up with me warts and all. Thank you for telling me that you love me, that I'm beautiful and sexy every day. Thank you for not giving up on us even when times were tough. Thank you for teaching me to get out of my comfort zone. Thank you for all the laughter. Thank you for introducing me to the world of business and entrepreneurship. Thank you for leaping into the unknown so readily with me each time. Thank you especially for co-parenting with me so I can write this book, launch my business and live my dream life. You are the best!

And thank you to my girls. Léna and Clémence. There are no words to explain just how much I love you both. I have tears in my eyes as I write this. You are the most incredible, amazing, funny, intelligent and loving people. I want you to know that you can do or be anything. I want you to remember that anything is possible. I want you to live your best life, never doubting what you are capable of. If you ever doubt, come back here and read this. Thank you for being the most incredible daughters anyone could ever ask for. Thank you for teaching me to be a better mum. Thank you for all your love, hugs and kisses. You are so so loved.

Thank you to all the women I work with - especially to my Life Reboot Campers, who have become my family, my sisters, my community, my passion. Thank you for believing in me. Thank you for showing up. Thank you for doing the work and for creating the butterfly effect in your world and in the whole world.

Thank you to the incredible women who offered to read the first (very messy) draft of this book, and for giving me their feedback -

Tracey, Olivia, Denise, Jac and Jennifer - any mistakes are very much my own.

And finally thank you reader for buying this book, for taking a chance on me and wanting to make a positive change in your life, which indirectly makes a positive change to the world around you. If you liked this book please please do go and review it on Amazon (and anywhere else online!), it makes the world of difference to me, but also to others wondering whether to buy it. And of course do tell all your friends about it too.

At this precise moment in time I am not active on social media, so if you want to keep up with me (which I would LOVE!) then do sign up to my mailing list to get my blog posts and emails: www.SophieLeBrozec.com/newsletter

Big love,
Sophie xx

About the author

Sophie Le Brozec is a Brit married to a Frenchman (hence the fancy-sounding name) and mum of two half British-half French daughters, two rescue dogs and two rescue cats. She did a degree in French and Spanish at Liverpool John Moores University, UK then moved to Nice, France for 3 months...she finally moved back to the UK 12 years later. Nearly 5 years in London had Sophie longing for sunshine again and so she moved to the tropical island of Mauritius, with her husband and two daughters. Despite knowing no one there and having never been there before. Mark Twain said that heaven was copied after Mauritius and Sophie is inclined to agree.

Sophie's husband Ben jokes that Sophie has done every job that exists except prostitution. She is now delighted to be doing what she loves best - helping women live their best and happiest life. She does this mainly through her free blog content (sign up to her mailing list here so you don't miss out: www.SophieLeBrozec.com/newsletter) and through her paid online course and community, Life Reboot Camp (sign up here www.SophieLeBrozec.com/camp-book to join at a reduced rate for readers of this book).

Sophie is passionate about giving back so 10% of her profits go to a variety of charities, and for every paid space in Life Reboot Camp sold she gives away a free space to a woman in need.

Sophie has a dream that through her work women all over the world will live a happier, more fulfilled life, which will ripple through to their spouses, kids, siblings, colleagues, neighbours, friends and society as a whole. Because she also believes that anything is possible.

Printed in Great Britain
by Amazon